Teaching Across Cultures in the University ESL Program

Edited by Patricia Byrd

Annotated Bibliography and
Reference Section
Edited by Janet C. Constantinides

National Association for Foreign Student Affairs, 1986

The National Association for Foreign Student Affairs (NAFSA) is a non-profit membership association that provides training, information, and other educational services to professionals in the field of international educational exchange.

Support for this publication was provided by the Student Support Services Division of the U.S. Information Agency through a grant to the NAFSA Field Service.

Copies may be ordered from the Publications Order Desk, National Association for Foreign Student Affairs, 1860 19th Street, N.W., Washington, D.C. 20009

ISBN 0-912207-17-5

Table of Contents

III: Teacher Solutions and Applications

Reference Section

Notes

INTRODUCTION

Barriers to Cross-Cultural Communication in English-as-a-Second-Language Programs in the United States

PATRICIA BYRD
Georgia State University

When I began teaching English as a Second Language (ESL) some 15 years ago, most ESL programs were focused on the teaching of the English language as a set of linguistic skills. Over the years, we have recognized that language learning involves much more than grammar or vocabulary or pronunciation. To become effective users of American English, students must also learn to communicate within the context of American culture. Thus programs and individual teachers have been making adjustments in the traditional curricula and courses of ESL programs to add cultural understanding to the linguistic core.

ESL programs must deal with numerous barriers to this goal of cultural adjustment and true communicative competence; major among these are the low English proficiency of most students, their fears of indoctrination, their narrowly focused goals, and insufficient training in cultural differences or cross-cultural communication on the part of many teachers. In addition to these barriers, the ESL program must also achieve cultural understanding and acceptance within classes that mix together representatives of many different cultures. For this last reason, ESL programs must have not only the limited goal of orientation to United States culture but also the broader goal of general understanding of ourselves and others as cultural beings and as cultural representatives.

In 1984, the Regents Publishing Company discovered in a survey of ESL teachers that only 12 percent of them taught advanced students. Nearly 75 percent had students who were called "beginners." Not too many terms ago, I knew an ESL student who wanted cereal and milk for breakfast. He went to the grocery store and bought a carton of milk and a package that he assumed had cereal in it—it was the right shape and had pictures of a happy family playing with a cat. When he shook the box, it sounded like cereal. He thought that the cereal was terrible, but he had not expected much from U.S. food. After about a month, he learned the word for "cat" and realized that he had been eating dried cat food for breakfast. For such students, abstract discussions of cultural awareness and adjustment are not yet a possibility.

Even as we discover ways to help our ESL students better understand the culture in which they are studying, we must accept as real their (and their family's and their government's) fears that we will attempt to turn them into Americans through a program of indoctrination and brainwashing. This fear is not to be hastily put aside or rejected as naive. Political and religious thinkers and leaders have long worried about the subversion of their young people through the vehicle of language learning. In the late 18th century, the imperial historiographer of the Ottoman Empire, Ahmed Asim Efendi, had this to say on the subject (Lewis 1982: 57):

> Certain sensualists, naked of the garment of loyalty, from time to time learned politics from them. Some, desirous of learning their language, took French teachers, acquired their idiom and prided themselves . . . on their uncouth talk. In this way the French were able to insinuate Frankish customs into the hearts and endear their modes of thought to the minds of some people of weak mind and shallow faith. The sober-minded and farsighted and the ambassadors of the other states all saw the danger of the situation. Full of alarm and disapproval, they reviled and condemned these things both implicitly and explicity, and gave forewarning of the evil consequences to which their activities would give rise. This malicious crew and abominable band were full of cunning, first sowing the seed of their politics in the soil of the hearts of the great ones of the state, then by incitement and seduction to their ways of thought, undermining—God preserve us—the principles of the Holy Law.

Less than fifty years later, Sultan Mahmud II himself warned students at the opening of a medical school that learning a new language was to be for strictly limited purposes (Lewis 1982: 87):

> You will study scientific medicine in French . . . my purpose in having you taught French is not to educate you in the French language; it is to teach you scientific medicine and little by little to take it into our language . . . therefore work hard to acquire a knowledge of medicine from your teachers and strive by degrees to adopt it into Turkish and give it currency in our language. . . .

Students and their sponsors continue to have limited and narrowly focused goals for language learning. While administrators and teachers see a need for cultural orientation, students may not only be afraid of being indoctrinated but also wonder if their time would not be better spent in studying for the Test of English as a Foreign Language (TOEFL).

One irony of the TOEFL-preparation visions of ESL is that TOEFL itself carries a heavy burden of cultural information. Even TOEFL preparation courses must deal with United States culture as the students learn to answer multiple choice questions that are set in United States contexts. Here are two examples of TOEFL questions from ETS's *Listening to TOEFL: Test Kit 2* that have relatively simple language problems except for the cultural load they carry. In the listening comprehension selection, a question seems to be about the ability to understand directions. A voice says, "Take a right on Main Street." The student has four choices for statements that mean the same thing—a. The writer's book is titled *Main Street*, b. Turn right at Main Street, c. We're going straight to Maine, d. They took a ton of rye bread." For the American writers of the item, the words <u>Main Street</u> must resonate with typical U.S.ness. For a foreign student with little or no experience of United States small towns or American literature of the early 20th century, it is possible that the question is confusing at the wrong point. The second example is from the grammar section. The student is given a sentence with four sections underlined. The task is to decide which part of the sentence is wrong.

Edna Ferber <u>told</u> the <u>story</u> of her <u>life</u> in two <u>book</u>.

The question is about noun plurals, but a student must plow through <u>Edna Ferber</u> before getting around to the relatively simple grammatical problem.

Since we cannot hope to familiarize our students with the entire range of United States culture and history and literature, we are left with the task of teaching the test-taking skill of learning to guess our way around information that we do not know. But to first decide that <u>Edna Ferber</u> is not important information a student must at least be able to decide that the words represent a given name and that they are functioning as the subject of the sentence but are not important to the answering of the question.

TOEFL is not a pure language test. Nor should it be. In fact, it cannot possibly be devoid of cultural content. The point is that in trying to teach students to be prepared for TOEFL and for communication in general, as well as academic society in the United States, an ESL program has some difficult choices to make about what needs to be done and about what it is humanly possible to do. Moreover, students and sponsors need to be helped to realize that the best possible preparation for success as a student and as a sojourner is a program of instruction that includes cultural orientation as part of the language instruction.

In addition to the barriers that are erected by students and sponsors, ESL programs have problems that result from the cultural innocence of its faculty members. At this point in our history, the typical ESL classroom teacher is a woman with a degree in the Teaching of English as a Second Language (TESL) or linguistics who has had some experience of living overseas. Her typical students are Third World men who have had little experience with modern liberated women. Just this restricted description suggests that the ESL program has important responsibilities in preparing the teachers and students to work productively together. Orientation programs cannot be aimed just at students but also must be planned as part of the in-service training for teachers.

At a session of the 1984 NAFSA Annual Conference in Snowmass, Colorado, participants were asked to list the issues raised by the conflict of one cultural group with another within an ESL program or on a college or university campus. Fourteen problems were identified: (1) political groups, (2) learning styles, (3) study skills, (4) values of respect—how respect is signaled to a teacher, (5) friendship styles, (6) prejudice, (7) "flaunting" money, (8) different family styles—different child-rearing styles, (9) styles of dress, (10) acceptable classroom behavior based on age as well as broader cultural values, (11) religious differences, (12) language barriers, (13) foreign students not wanting foreign teachers. The fourteenth is the perennial ESL topic: complaints by students and faculty about body odors of students with bathing, clothes-washing, and use-of-deodorant/perfume habits different from those of middle-class, educated Americans. The solutions suggested by that group focused on program responsibilities for cross-cultural training for faculty and staff as well as for the foreign students.

The articles in this collection were selected on the basis of abstracts submitted in response to a national call-for-papers. The original intent had been to have discussions of four topics, three of which are covered by this volume: (1) background discussions of relevant issues, (2) programs developed at the institutional or program level, and (3) materials and methods developed by individual teachers. It had been hoped to include as the fourth topic discussions of work being done with students from particular cultural backgrounds. When the call-for-papers did not bring forth an adequate number of abstracts in this area, the editorial committee decided to delay inclusion of that topic for future revisions of the book.

While the materials in this collection cannot attempt to solve all of the problems suggested by the participants in the 1984 Annual NAFSA Conference, the reader will find that ESL programs in the United States have been actively developing programs and courses to address the cultural needs of ESL students and their teachers. The articles in Section I address more general and theoretical aspects of the topic while in Section II descriptions are given of the cross-cultural communication and orientation programs developed by four institutions. In Section III, individual teachers discuss materials and courses that they have developed in response to various needs they have found among their students. The volume ends with an annotated bibliography which is followed by the reference section for the articles themselves. Since a number of the articles made reference to the same sources, it was decided to collect all references in one place. It was also thought that a collected reference section might be easier to use for the reader and for those carrying out additional research projects.

One of the most striking features of this collection taken as a whole is the variety of solutions found by the different ESL programs and their teachers. Everything from academic discussions of the characteristics of culture shock to having lunch with United States elementary school children is being tried. An important lesson to be learned from the materials is that different institutions in different settings with different students will need to find unique, localized solutions within the bounds set by an understanding of what culture and cross-cultural communication mean. It is the hope of the authors and editors that this collection will help other programs and other teachers as they develop cross-cultural orientation that will benefit their students.

The authors are teachers, scholars, and administrators from institutions large and small, private and public, from all around the United States. A major editorial principle was to allow each author his/her own voice and style within the general framework of U.S. academic prose. The volume, thus, speaks in the many unique voices of ESL.

Numerous members of the National Association for Foreign Student Affairs (NAFSA) have helped in the creation of this volume, among them the leadership of the Association of Teachers of English as a Second Language (ATESL) from 1983-1985. During these two years, the leadership conceived a new direction for ATESL publications as it designed and began a series of volumes on topics of interest to the profession. The first of these is the *Administration of Intensive English Programs*, edited by Ralph Pat Barrett. The second is *Foreign Teaching Assistants in U.S. Universities*, edited by Kathleen M. Bailey, Frank Pialorsi, and Jean Zukowski-Faust. Other topics under consideration include testing and teacher training. The guiding purpose of the series is to have a collection of discussions, both theoretical and practical, that can improve the quality of instruction provided for foreign students who are studying ESL or EFL with the goal of entering U.S. academic programs.

Special thanks go to Mary Peterson, director of the Field Service Program, and Virginia Louisell, director of Information Services, at the NAFSA Central Office in Washington, D.C. Their interest in ESL as a vital part of international educational exchange demonstrates once again the concern that NAFSA has for interdisciplinary, cooperative, and integrative approaches to cross-cultural communication and education.

William Powell, Florida State University, David Eskey, University of Southern California, and Mark Landa, University of Minnesota, served as readers in the final stages of editing. Their recommendations helped the authors be more exact in their presentations and guided the editor in making decisions about the ordering of materials. Dave Eskey provided the final title for the collection.

Janet C. Constantinides, University of Wyoming, and Donna Rice, SUNY-Buffalo, gave generously of their time, energy, and experience in cross-cultural communication by serving as readers and advisers to the editor. They worked both in the initial stages of selecting abstracts and designing the organization of the volume and also in the final stages of reviewing the submitted papers. While the authors are ultimately responsible for their own ideas and the editor is responsible for the final selection and ordering of the materials, Janet and Donna should be given major credit for helping to bring this volume to reality.

BACKGROUND DISCUSSIONS

Acculturation or Enculturation: Foreign Students in the United States

P. B. NAYAR
University of South Carolina

No one will deny that English is the closest thing we have today to a world language. "It is the language of diplomacy, the predominant language in which mail is written, the principal language of aviation and of radio broadcasting, the first language of nearly three hundred million people and an additional language of perhaps that many more" (Conrad and Fishman 1977). That and the fact that native English-speaking countries are also among the world's most developed countries have resulted in a modern version of the "white man's burden." Most of the onus of educating the developing world has also, in a way, fallen on the English-speaking countries. Statistics quoted in Conrad and Fishman (1977) indicate that the United States is by far the most popular host country for both nonimmigrant and immigrant overseas students, and that nearly three quarters of foreign students continue to be from Afro-Asia and Latin America, with students from Afro-Asia showing a greater rate of growth. *The Washington Post* (September 5, 1984) shows a record enrollment of 338,894 foreign students in United States colleges for the 1983-84 school year (almost 3 percent of the total college enrollment), with the biggest enrollments from Taiwan, Iran, Nigeria, and Malaysia.

Many of these students may have theoretically met the minimal standards of English proficiency expected of them before arrival here. However, it is also true that quite a large number of them will also need and/or seek instruction in English in the various ESL institutions in this country. During the course of their sojourn in the United States, English is not merely their language for academic communication, but also their main medium of social interaction with the multicultural academic community, and the only medium of interaction with their hosts.

1

The words communication and interaction perhaps provide a vital cue for a very important factor for the successful realization of the overseas students' sojourn objectives—their acculturation to the ways of the host country. The main responsiblity for this acculturation has fallen, and rightly, too, on the language teacher. The English-teaching programs have had to incorporate a culture component to transform the sojourners from mere "English-literate aliens" to their rightful role of welcome guests. In a sense, language teachers have always taught the culture of the target language community both implicitly and explicitly, the emphasis perhaps being more on Culture than on culture. (The "C" and "c" notion has been used by Lafayette (1979). Culture was the domain of historians, artistes, and litterateurs, while culture used to be the concern of anthropologists.)

Although linguists, anthropologists, and sociologists may have been vaguely aware of the complex connection between culture and language, it was the work of Edward Sapir and Benjamin Lee Whorf that really made people perceive the reciprocal implicational relationship between language and culture (see Sapir 1949 and Whorf 1956). However, more recent developments in anthropology, sociology, philosophy, linguistics, communications, education, and several related fields in humanities have culminated in the inclusion of cultural competence as a part of linguistic, social, and communicative competence, and have produced the much-needed impetus for the language teacher for a more purposeful teaching of culture by putting culture and its role in the right perspective.

Before going into the complex issues of cross-cultural problems and their implications on the nature of the culture component, it might be useful to look briefly at two things: First, how can we have broad yet concrete guidelines as to what we mean by culture in the present context? Secondly, how is what we call culture generally seen to relate to language teaching and learning?

Culture has been one of the most widely used but vaguely defined concepts. Kroeber and Kluckhohn (1963) have probably made the most exhaustive study of the meaning of culture by tracing its semantic history and by looking at hundreds of definitions of culture, but state in their introduction that "indeed a few sociologists and even anthropologists have already, either implicitly or explicitly, rejected the concept of culture as so broad as to be useless in scientific discourse or too tinged with valuation." The anthropological sense of the term is well brought out by Harris and Moran (1979): "In the classical anthropological sense, culture refers to the cumulative deposit of knowledge, beliefs, values, religion, customs, and mores acquired by a group of people and passed on from generation to generation." They further supplement this by adding that "It is also communicable knowledge, learned behavioral traits that are shared by participants in social groups and manifested in their institutions." But culture, as it concerns us here, should also take into account the sociological component of the rules and presuppositions of social interaction, communo-syncratic conventions of nonverbal behavior, standards of kinesics and proxemics as well as the individual's perceived status

2

and role relationships in society. This is perhaps what Brooks (1968) has in mind when he talks about culture in the language class as "the individual's role in the unending kaleidoscope of life situations of every kind and the rules and models for attitude and conduct in them."

Several factors have contributed to an increased awareness of the ways in which culture relates to language, particularly in a cross-cultural and hence cross-linguistic situation. These factors have a direct bearing on the rationale and direction of the teaching of culture. Nearly half a century ago Whorf suggested the possibility of language predisposing and conditioning the user's cognitive structure (see Whorf 1956). It would therefore follow that experience is filtered, organized, and modified by one's perceptual mechanism, conditioned by culture and its exponent, language. Brislin (1981) describes in some detail this aspect and its implication on interaction. Somewhat similar is the "screening function" of culture that Hall (1976) mentions. Moreover, the last decade has seen a shift in the goal of language teaching from linguistic competence to communicative competence. Communicative competence can be defined as a set of strategies or creative procedures for realizing the value of linguistic elements in contexts of use, an ability to make sense as a participant in a discourse, spoken or written, by the skillful deployment of shared knowledge of code resources and rules of language use (Widdowson 1979). It therefore presumes not merely grammatically correct but culturally acceptable ways of using language (Robinett 1978) involving various kinds of socio-linguistic information and subsuming competence in pragmatics, stylistics, and discourse strategies. As Watson (1977) explains:

> Learning the structure of language and learning how to create well-formed phrases and sentences which violate no linguistic dicta is not the same as learning to use that language in social interaction. In order to communicate effectively, to interpret intelligently, and to perceive the social processes underlying interaction, learning a language must include learning the *rules for speaking* in a given community. The rules of speaking I take to be the nexus between language learning and culture learning.

Watson goes on to state that though Singaporeans and Californians share a grammatical knowledge of English, they may not share the same interactional rules, which are not linguistic but social, dictated by the culture. To cite an example of social competence, although an Arab may well be able to produce the sentence "How is your family?" he may have to "learn" to talk about the welfare of the family in public to casual acquaintances. There is, however, more than just learning social rules involved in the understanding of discourse. Take for instance the dialogue:

A: Do you know what day it is?
B: All under control. I'm taking her out to dinner and she should have got the present by now.

To make sense out of B's response, first of all the response has to be deemed relevant to A's question (for the concept of "relevance" in language, see

Smith and Wilson 1979) since B doesn't say anything like "Yes, I do" or "It's Tuesday." Assuming that it is a relevant response, one still needs a lot of non-linguistic information to make sense of it: that A and B are friends; that A knows that it is B's wedding anniversary; that a wedding anniversary is important; that such matters are discussed between friends; that it is customary to give one's wife a present on the occasion; that taking her out to dinner is a desirable way of celebrating; that not doing anything about it would create problems, etc. A Third World student may have passed his TOEFL or GMAT with distinction but may not have a clue as to what is going on here. Without shared cultural information, plain linguistic information may not communicate at all.

Guthrie (1975) shows remarkable parallels between learning to speak a second language and learning to live in a second culture, as a reminder that communication and culture are inseparable and that a major component of differences in culture is differences in communication. His nine-point table is summarized below.

1. Both language and culture are acquired early and are relatively fixed by the age of five.

2. New language and new culture patterns are learned more easily by children than by adults.

3. First language structures habits of thinking and first culture determines habits of valuing.

4. A new language has a new set of sounds and a new culture has a new range of space and distance relationships.

5. Interference errors from native language (L1) and native culture (C1) are found in the second language (L2) and the new culture (C2).

6. An accent remains which reveals the first language, just as patterns of first culture distort and influence the expression of the new.

7. In instances of severe frustration or illness, one reverts to first language and when life is difficult one reverts to patterns of first culture relationships.

8. Deepest feelings are best expressed in L1 and deepest values are best expressed in overt behavior patterns that are long standing.

9. One ponders his deepest personal values and problems in the words and concepts of his first language, and one feels most deeply in terms of his first learned value system.

To these nine, the following six correlations could be added.

1. There is often regressive interference from L2 on L1 and from C2 on C1.

2. A learner often has a restricted code in specific purpose instrumental language learning, and one adopts only restricted aspects of C2 in limited interaction.

3. Motivation to learn a second language flags with the attaining of a communicative competence perceived adequate by the learner, and motivation for learning a second culture flags with minimal acceptability in the target culture (plateau effect).

4

4. The strategies of acquisition versus learning are applicable to both L1 and L2 and C1 and C2.

5. A "hidden curriculum" effect (Brislin 1977) obtains in both situations.

6. Contrastive analysis can predict a hierarchy of interference/facilitation features cross-linguistically as well as cross-culturally.

Linguistic competence without corresponding cultural competence can seriously impair communication. Anyone experienced in cross-cultural encounters will have, at one time or the other, come across embarrassing situations where the parties in an interaction will use the same linguistic code fluently but will either not communicate at all or will miscommunicate. The BBC once showed an interesting situation in which an Indian immigrant had called on the British headmistress of his teenage daughter to talk about the daughter's career. As the discussion progressed, there was more and more language but less and less communication. The Indian's parents-know-best-what-is-best-for-children attitude clashed with the let-the-child-be-what-she-wants-to-be attitude of the headmistress. The Indian resented what he thought was the school's incursion into his parental authority and family security, and the Britisher was put out by the intransigent Indian's meddling with the life of a British subject. The Indian's "No" in place of the usual British "Yes, but . . ." was interpreted as uncooperative rudeness. The firm suggestion of the Britisher with a "Don't you think . . ." was interpreted as a yes/no question by the Indian. And one could see that the whole process was a non-starter as meaningful communication. Gumperz (1978) gives a detailed analysis of a somewhat similar conversation between a college entrant in Britain who was a Punjabi speaker and his British female interlocutor. It thus appears that a cultural component is not only advisable but essential in an ESL program.

In the United States, it is necessary to identify and differentiate between at least three types of ESL situations, and ESL teachers in America might encounter at least three types of situations with different culture instruction needs. The three are (1) teaching English to the ethnic minorities in the United States, (2) teaching English to fresh immigrants, and (3) teaching English to sojourners of various types. The first group are Americans who happen to have a native language other than English (e.g. Hispanics) and will have varying degrees of acculturation and assimilation (Jaramillo 1973). These are probably the people involved in the notion of bilingual education in a pluralistic society. The second group consists of the continual waves of immigrants from all over the world who have the avowed intention of making the United States their permanent home. They have virtually no acculturation at all, but would want total assimilation into and identification with everything American. What they need is enculturation. Acculturation to them is only a preliminary to total enculturation and assimilation.

The third group consists of sojourners, who come and reside here for varying periods of relatively short duration. They have specific objectives for their residence, most commonly higher education. Naturally their residential status is different, as is their motivation for learning English. It is with this third group that we are concerned here. Their acculturation requirements are both qualitatively and quantitatively different from those of the other two. There are, however, four important factors that seem to favor explicit teaching of cultural elements. Firstly, the sojourners, by and large, are cognitively mature enough to be explicitly taught; secondly, as McLeod (1980) points out, they just do not have enough time to go through the experiential learning process of "hypothesis formation and testing procedure"; thirdly, apart from core culturemes, their acculturation priorities are best determined by their sojourn objectives; and finally, unorganized and unplanned enculturation may even be inadvisable as it would create problems of readjustment when they return home.

It is very tempting to look at this cross-cultural situation in terms of a tentative but interesting analogy from sports. Culture itself is the complicated sport and the name of the non-competitive game is cross-cultural encounter. The host country is the home team and the sojourners are the visitors. The home team has several advantages: Firstly, they are homogeneous and hence have a better team spirit; secondly, they are on their home ground and so more secure; thirdly, the game is more or less played by their rules; and lastly, if the game is not properly played, the casualities and injuries are almost invariably suffered by the visitors. The visitors, like the medieval European Crusaders, are a heterogeneous group with widely different concepts of the rules of the game and widely different interests and motivations in playing it. The object of the game is for the visitors to join ranks with the home team. The language teachers function variously as managers, coaches, medics, etc., for the visitors and also as referees, facilitators, and promoters. They are, thus, in a way, in charge of the whole game, and should, ideally, know the rules both teams go by.

Several attempts have been made to evolve a functional taxonomy for the various aspects of culture that are directly involved in cross-cultural situations, both by "culturologists" and by writers of textbooks on the teaching of culture. The five different types of Brooks (1968), Nostrand's Emergent Model (Seelye 1968), Jaramillo's (1973) five components, Robinett's (1978) cultural features taken from various acknowledged sources, Ruhly's (1976) iceberg-analogy model, the eight variables of Samovar and Porter (1976), and the four themes of Condon and Yousef (1975) are some examples from culturologists. Two examples from textbooks are the aspects of culture presented in Johnson (1979) and in Levine and Adelman (1982). A very convenient model for language teachers for considering cross-cultural contact and adjustment problems is that of Harris and Moran (1979), whose ten categories are (1) communication and language, (2) dress and appearance, (3) food and feeding habits, (4) time and time consciousness, (5) rewards and recognitions, (6) relationships, (7) values and norms, (8) sense of self and space, (9) mental process and learning, (10) beliefs and attitudes. These categories are really not discrete, independent units, but interrelated parameters.

6

It is impossible to make any generalizations about foreign students for obvious reasons of forbiddingly large ethnic, sociological, religious, economic, and developmental diversities. The emphasis in the discussion that follows is on foreign students from the Third World Afro-Asian countries, for the cultures they represent are qualitatively more different than those from European or Latin American countries. Although the cross-cultural examples and instances cited here will thus more directly refer to Afro-Asian countries, the general principles involved are applicable to all foreign students in the United States. (The concept of the Third World here is more socio-technological than political; see Condon and Yousef 1975.)

Even though the diversities among even the developing Afro-Asian countries are too many to permit many meaningful generalizations, there are several common denominators. First, the relatively uniform sojourn objective of the pursuit of higher education tends to standardize, in some measure, their language and culture needs; second, the intracultural differences among the sojourners from non-technocratic countries are probably not as large or at least not functionally as important as the intercultural differences between them and their hosts. In other words, at the level with which we are concerned, the qualitative differences between them and their hosts are more significant than differences among them. Third, many of the Third World sojourners come from Afro-Asian countries with composite, complex, and multicultural societies where an intercultural perspective is endemic and where monolingualism is the exception rather than the rule. This implies that what they need is not just an orientation to a *second culture* but knowledge about those aspects of *American culture* that directly concern them and help in coping outside the support system of their own culture. Fourth, the ghost of "the white man's burden" is still alive in a more subtle and subversive way (Bochner 1977), and economically and educationally deprived people are most likely to be labeled primitive, uncivilized, and uncultured. This has the effect of making people from traditional Third World cultures fearful of domination and of the eventual extinction of their cultures. They thus get very protectively defensive of their own culture. Finally, their initial impression of America and attitudes and affective reactions towards American culture, values, and ways of life are likely to be somewhat similar. A sojourner does not bother to seek out the "deep structure" (Condon and Yousef 1975) of cultural values. His initial impressions are from surface realizations. For instance, "A McDonald's hamburger may offer us a rich diet of American values: efficiency, sameness, quantification. *Playboy* magazine has been analyzed to demonstrate a variety of American themes, including, as a colleague noted, standardization and the belief that bigger is better!" (Condon and Yousef 1975). The sojourners are also victims of a syndrome that most cultures cannot help—stereotyping. There are very few people who have been as vitriolically stereotyped as the "ugly American"—pushy, impatient, supercilious, patronizing, and self-righteous. Besides, these sojourners' awareness of American culture is very likely gained from cops-robbers-violence television movies and sleazy, escapist soap operas that America generously exports abroad. In a survey conducted by the author among students in the English Program for Internationals at the University of South Carolina, a significant number of students admitted they had thought of the United States as a crime-ridden country consisting of built-up city centers with skyscrapers and huge cowboy-country ranches.

Now, for the profile of the other side. There is some truth in the fact that Americans appear to foreigners to be overbearing, patronizing, culturally naive and myopic, ethnocentric, and in general ignorant and unconcerned about other cultures and ways of life. Trifonovitch (1977) talks about the unconscious attitude of Americans towards other cultures. He says that this attitude reveals itself abroad in such statements as "They don't even speak English there" or "I know how to teach them English. I taught mentally retarded children English in the States before I came here." Americans also often tend to equate a foreigner's English language competence with mental and intellectual development. Again, an American's evaluation of the English language competence of a foreigner is not compatible with his evaluation of his own competence in a foreign language. An American who speaks some Malay, for instance, will be rated well over a native Malay with fluent English. This attitude is perhaps not unrealistic in that competence in English is more important to the Malay than vice versa. But this is an attitude that is very detrimental to equal status contact, which is vitally necessary for making the sojourner feel secure. An invariable result of cultural naivety and myopia is a belief in the universal infallibility of one's own way of life. The author was once asked by an American colleague about the significance of the color worn on the forehead of Indian women. Realizing the complications of explaining Hindu traditions to someone used to only Judeo-Christian traditions, I tried to simplify things by answering half-jokingly that it was something similar to the color worn on the lips by American women. But the colleague's next remark nearly took the wind out of my sails. Showing impatient annoyance at my apparent stupidity, he remarked, "But that's on the lips!" Another instance of ethnocentrism is the American reaction to Afro-Asian names. The sojourner is made to feel embarrassed, self-conscious, and somehow apologetic for not having a name that is euphonious to the American ear. If it does not conform to English phonotactics it is dubbed unpronounceable and unrememberable and is, if possible, Anglicized. Similarly, all foreigners are expected to conform to the American nomenclature with a given name, middle initial, and a surname constituting a full name, and are also supposed to have a street address and a zip code in their countries! Even statements that are complimentary on the surface like "You speak our language beautifully!" come through as patronizing in an it's-a-marvel-you-folks-can-achieve-that attitude. Harris and Moran (1979) give a fairly exhaustive list of mainstream cultural features of the United States. More interesting are Hsu's (1969) nine postulates, each of which has several corollaries embodying the basic working philosophy of the United States. In the final postulate Hsu implies

8

that the U.S. has a mission to spread Americanism, which is the acme and apogee of progress in the world, and that America will unconditionally help those who accept its superiority, but will, if necessary, destroy any obstructions to Americanization for the good of the world.

Situations and instances of cross-cultural miscommunications along with their etiology and theoretical explanations have been discussed by many people, notably by Condon and Yousef (1975), Seelye (1974), Harris and Moran (1979), Hoopes and Ventura (1979), and Brislin (1981). Most of these discussions, however, present the converse situation of what we are concerned with here, that is, the situation of American sojourners abroad. But the principles involved in them are applicable to sojourners in America, too. Although the Third World students in America are too diverse for a united approach to their problems, some generalized areas of conflict can be traced. Most of the Third World students come from hierarchically structured, androcentric societies with extended family systems which contrast with the highly mobile and "sexually liberated" American society with a nuclear family system and egalitarian values. Even their priority of family loyalties are the reverse of those in America (Trifonovitch 1977). Another area of substantial difference is in time and space orientation. The Euro-American monochronic (one thing at a time) concept of time does not correspond to the Third World's polychronic approach to time (Hall 1976). This is illustrated in the stereotypical coining by Euro-American expatriates of such phrases as "Melanesian time" in the South Pacific (meaning vague and unpunctual), "native appointment" (one not intended to be kept) in Ethiopia, "Indian punctuality," etc. The difference in space orientation and its implications on house and home values of different cultures are clearly illustrated in Condon and Yousef (1975). Generally, Americans find Third World societies very "people-oriented," and they in turn are puzzled by the American obsession with exclusiveness and privacy. Again, Third World sojourners find American social interaction conspicuously formal and the tradition of "polite social lying" just to be nice to each other embarrassingly confusing. Because of a different set of values for interpersonal relations, American friendliness is mistaken for friendship, which in Third World societies involves totally different mutual obligations. The conventions of nonverbal communication and the relation between verbal and nonverbal communication are additional areas that are intensely culture specific. Finally, the differences in the strategies and processes of communicating can lead to miscommunication. American culture is a relatively low-context culture, while Afro-Asian cultures are relatively high-context cultures (Hall 1976). In low-context communication, the majority of information is contained in the explicit code, whereas in high-context communication the majority of information is either in the physical context or internalized in the person (Harris and Moran 1979). To an outsider, Americans often seem to be stating the obvious and they seem to look for meaning only in *what is said.*

The adjustment problems of foreign students are basically of two types: encounters with a different culture and coping with the differences. The first has to do with the general problem of finding oneself in a new environment outside the comfortable cocoon and support system of one's own culture. This is known as *culture shock* (Brein and David 1971, Harris and Moran 1979, Casse 1979, Brislin 1981). "It is analogous to the experience of sensory deprivation, an experimental condition in which one is progressively denied sensation from his various sense organs until, sensing nothing, he becomes frightened and disoriented" (Guthrie 1975). The shock culminates in the "hostility stage" (McLeod 1980) of the encounter and leads to "resistance reaction" (Seelye 1968) and catatonia. The situation is aggravated by the sojourner's sense of inferiority caused by his communicative inadequacy and by the perceived superiority of the hosts. The culture-shocked person feels incompetent, ignorant, and even infantile (Hall 1976). One effective way of dealing with and softening the cultural shock in the author's experience is to use a host culture-competent foreigner as a culture mediator in the early stages of contact. The sojourners often feel less insecure with someone they feel is "one of us," and having himself at one time survived the culture shock, the mediator can establish greater empathy with new foreigners and win their "confidence." Ultimately, the effects of cultural shock will be assuaged only by time and perhaps by some other factors like the sojourner's intercultural experience, cognitive and behavioral flex, interpersonal sensitivity, etc. (Redden 1975). It is important that the teachers should try to impart a sympathetic but not a defensive view of the target culture.

The second problem of coping with and learning to live with the differences is of more direct concern to the language teacher. Here again, the cultural class areas fall into two sub-systems:

1. Some aspects of life and values are perceived by the foreigners as different and deviant from their own. These aspects amuse or disturb them but do not involve them. Some examples of these are the obsession with physical fitness and exercising, dieting, American child-rearing practices, pet mania, political attitudes, etc. Whether the sojourner understands them, likes them, or adopts them is only marginally relevant. These are low-priority areas for the teacher and need be dealt with only if the students show or express interest in them. These aspects, however, are very useful as pourparlers for cultural instruction as they are fairly "neutral" and students can discuss them without any serious affective involvement.

2. There are some other areas that affect and directly involve the sojourners. These aspects should form the nitty-gritty of cultural instruction. The teacher has two main tasks here. The first task is to identify and establish the general as well as specific goals of culture instruction and establish a priority, taking into account the sojourn objectives and the available time. Seelye (1974) describes seven different goals and a super goal for culture instruction, which is: "All students will develop the cultural understandings, attitudes, and performance skills needed to function appropriately within a society of the

10

target language and to communicate with the culture bearer." The first four of Seelye's specific goals—the sense, or functionality of culturally conditioned behavior, interaction of language and social variables, conventional behavior in common situations and cultural connotations of words and phrases—are immediately relevant to the needs of sojourners. Lafayette (1979) lists the following twelve cultural goals:

a. To recognize and/or interpret major geographical features of the target country (or countries).

b. To recognize and/or interpret major historical events pertaining to the target country.

c. To recognize and/or interpret major aesthetic monuments of the target culture, including architecture, literature, and the arts.

d. To recognize and/or interpret *active* everyday cultural patterns (e.g., eating, shopping, greeting people).

e. To recognize and/or interpret *passive* everyday cultural patterns (e.g., marriage, customs, education, politics).

f. To act appropriately in everyday situations.

g. To use appropriate common gestures.

h. To evaluate the validity of generalizations about foreign cultures.

i. To develop skills needed to research (i.e., locate and organize information about) culture.

j. To value different peoples and societies.

k. To recognize and/or interpret the culture of foreign language-related ethnic groups in the United States (e.g., Latinos, Franco-Americans).

l. To recognize and/or interpret the culture of additional countries that speak the foreign language (e.g., Canada, Haiti, Chile, Nicaragua). These are, no doubt, comprehensive, but goals 4 through 7, which Lafayette says belong to 'culture with a small "c" ' are the only ones that are fully relevent for sojourners.

Teachers can establish their own goals, but the following would provide a starting point:

a. To overcome the debilitating effects of culture shock that are detrimental to the fulfillment of sojourn objectives. (A depressed and alienated student does not learn well.)

b. To learn to adapt to the target culture and to overcome communication gaps, particularly in areas of immediate concern for sojourners—education and academic performance. (Knowledge of the educational system, requirements, academic role-relations and interaction, cultural connotations of vocabulary, and pragmatics.)

c. To understand, learn, and when necessary, conform to the ways of life and values of the hosts, to be a good guest, and to be so accepted by them. (Social competence—the sojourner should be liked and not just tolerated. Common decency demands a gesture of respect and gratitude for hospitality.)

d. To have an intercultural perspective and develop objectivity towards one's own culture and overcome the tendency to stereotype and prejudge; to

11

cultivate attitudinal and behavioral flex. (Personality enrichment is one of the goals of education.)

The nature, extent, and intensiveness of the culture knowledge needed would also depend on other factors like the duration of the sojourn, the amount of involvement in host country life, or even the particular area of study (perhaps the maximum for American literature and the minimum for computer science, etc.).

Having established the goals of cultural instruction, the teacher's next task is to analyze, isolate, and evaluate the culture components in the specific English-language needs of the students. This can be done as part of the general needs analysis of language instruction in the intensive English program. The English-language needs, for example, can be analyzed under three main categories:

a. Academic.

(1) To meet the admission requirements like passing TOEFL, GMAT, etc. The language component here is very important for sojourn objectives while the culture component is minimal. But there may still be some cultural factors in the aptitude part of the tests.

(2) To fulfill the academic requirements within the American educational system. The language content here is the most important for the sojourn objectives and the culture component is fairly large—being in a class with American peers; teacher-student relationships; Aristotelian logic and organization of ideas; "cheating" in classwork, etc.

b. Social.

This is the language category with the heaviest culture component—social interactional presuppositions; male-female relationships; partying; entertainment and recreational proclivities; personal relationships; nonverbal communication, etc.

c. Institutional.

This category has to do with the students' communicative abilities in dealing with the faceless bureaucracy and tedious routine of institutions. The language and culture components are fairly evenly matched here—shops, banks, restaurants, offices, etc.

Since one of the first groups of real people in the target culture that the students interact with are the English teachers, the teachers have additional non-pedagogic responsibilities. They have to be idealized representatives of the target culture as well as culture mediators. They have to be informal and friendly enough to make the students feel secure without appearing to be over-solicitous and patronizing. They have to be very careful not to make verbal or nonverbal *faux pas*. Nothing should be taken for granted in a cross-cultural situation involving widely different cultures. Possible pitfalls are too many. Even conversation fillers that appear harmless to an American can be potentially dangerous. A question like "Do you run?" may only cause an uncomprehending look on the face of a Third World sojourner. But "Do you fish?" when put to a high caste Indian can be perhaps be as offensive as "Do you

12

steal?" (In India, people who fish for a living generally belong to the "fisherman caste." To a highly caste-conscious, upper-caste Hindu like a Brahmin, it can be very offensive to be identified with a low-caste fisherman. Besides, the Brahmins are generally very strict vegetarians, for whom fish, meat, or even eggs are taboo and to whom association with any of these is distasteful. The Hindu caste system, though legally outlawed, is still very much a fact of everyday life in India even today.)

There are several realities of the Third World which may not even occur to average Americans: that people don't get married just because they love each other, or that they may not have a choice in the matter; that relaxation is not necessarily on a beach, or under palm trees, or in the mountains, or at the other end of a fishing rod; that one could live and die peacefully without a social security number or without even being aware of Jesus Christ; that people do not necessarily have to eat meat, or use toothpaste, toilet paper, or deodorant; that one can have and retain love and affection without overt osculatory or other proxemic or tactile demonstration of it; that the right to privacy may not be fundamental; that a teacher's private life may affect his/ her general credibility and acceptability; that students may not speak out even when they have a problem; that pursuit of personal material gains may only be of very low priority; that feelings of gratitude, obligation, indebtedness, appreciation, approbation, etc., do not have to be verbally expressed, but that such expression could even be taboo; that people do not need to have hobbies, or be conscious of their weight and figure; that life is not necessarily a race for achievement punctuated by weekends, holidays, retirement plans; and so on and so forth.

Successful ESL teachers should themselves develop an intercultural per-spective by taking care to learn as much about other cultures as posssible. They should free themselves from ethnocentrism, prejudice, and the tendency to stereotype, develop sensitivity to the culturemes of other cultures and learn to accept them as equal though different. They should believe in the funda-mental anthropological truth that no culture is necessarily superior, eschew any kind of cultural value judgement, and evolve teaching strategies, methods, and techniques that presume, ensure, and reinforce equal status contact. An improperly conceived culture component, particularly if agressively presented by overzealous teachers, will, regardless of the motives and attitudes of the teacher, make the foreign student feel threatened, confused, and generally inadequate. Instead of trying to learn and assimilate the host culture, he might shy away from it and actively resist acculturation. The ESL teachers should envision their roles as mediators and ambassadors of culture, and not as purveyors or disseminators, and never as imposers.

BACKGROUND DISCUSSIONS

A Framework for Cross-Cultural Analysis of Teaching Methods

PATRICIA R. FUREY
University of Pittsburgh

As Saville-Troike (1976), Paulston (1975), and others have pointed out, the EFL/ESL classroom is most often a culture contact setting where the students' cultural values and expectations of the learning process may diverge significantly from those of the teacher and curriculum designer. However, in selecting, implementing, and evaluating teaching methods we rarely pay sufficient attention to whether they are suitable for students whose notions of appropriate classroom behaviors and perceptions of student/teacher roles may differ from those providing their English training. This paper offers a framework to assist in determining the cross-cultural appropriateness of our teaching methods. Based on sources in foreign language (FL) teaching methodology, intercultural communications, and educational anthropology, it identifies and examines those factors in our methods and classroom practices which must be systematically compared with relevant features of our students' cultures in assessing the suitability of our instruction and suggesting where we must provide special orientation for those from a particular cultural background. Cultural values, the role of the teacher, modes of learning, teacher-student interaction patterns, and norms of interaction must all be considered in cross-cultural analysis. Examples of applications of the framework are provided with reference to selected cultural groups and current methodologies.

Teachers are so often concerned with teaching the body of material and series of skills explicitly designated in an official curriculum that they forget that students are also learning a hidden curriculum (Jackson 1968)—one

This article is a revised version of a paper presented at the 14th Annual TESOL Convention, 1980. The author wishes to thank Christina Paulston, Mary Bruder, Holly Deemer, Lionel Menasche, and Cathy Cake for comments on the earlier version, and to express appreciation to the many students, teachers, and colleagues who served as cultural informants.

15

which transmits the values, attitudes, and norms of behavior of the culture in which their education is set. But not only is the school a locus of broader culture learning, the classroom is its own subculture, and students must learn the highly patterned ways of thinking and behaving appropriate to it. Our adult ESL/EFL students come to our classes with their own sets of values, attitudes, and beliefs about the world in general and the classroom and learning in particular. This fact implies that along with linguistic, psychological, and pedagogical factors, we must also consider cultural differences as we select, implement, and evaluate our teaching methods and classroom practices and orient our students to them.

It is not my contention that cross-cultural comparison will predict the success or failure of particular methods, nor am I asserting that all differences are necessarily problems. I am not suggesting that we change our instructional strategies to conform to the ones our students are used to. As Philips (1972) points out, this is a disservice to those students who will eventually have to adapt to the learning patterns of the English-speaking culture. What should be useful is a framework specifying those features that provide a basis for cross-cultural comparison of teaching methods and classroom practices—a cultural checklist consisting of categories which the teacher or curriculum planner should investigate in order to anticipate possible sources of misunderstanding, conflict, or difficulty in the multicultural classroom.

The categories contained in the framework are drawn from three main sources. Many have emerged from my own experience and that of my colleagues at the English Language Institute, University of Pittsburgh. Others were suggested during interviews with EFL teachers having experience in teaching both in the U.S. and other cultures. Finally, literature in sociolinguistics, educational anthropology, and intercultural communication provided information contributing to the development of the framework.

Some of the categories, by their very nature, involve only the subculture of the classroom; others involve both the general culture and its parallels in the classroom subculture. The relationship between these two systems is an interesting one and needs further comment. Very often certain values, attitudes, and behavioral patterns of the general culture are directly reflected in and reinforced by the educational setting. On the other hand, there are many similarities in classrooms across societies which in numerous other respects are quite dissimilar. This probably has to do with the pervasive influence and leveling effect of Western thought on education throughout so much of the world. Also, of course, formal education is a phenomenon with certain inherent and universal features which supersede any particular cultural setting.

The framework offered here is a partial and tentative one. Its intent is to provide a scheme for thinking about cultural differences as they relate to what goes on in the ESL/EFL class. What is clearly needed is more data—systematic comparative research in pedagogy and classroom practice which will enable us to better understand cultural aspects of instruction and eventually develop a more complete and refined model for cross-cultural analysis of teaching

16

Table 1
Cultural Values

General Culture	Culture of the Classroom
Differences in:	Differences in:
A. Individualism/Group orientation	A. Individual competition, sense of privacy about individual work, striving for individual achievement Group cooperation, sharing among students, desire not to stand apart from group or lose face vis-a-vis group
B. Attitudes toward use of time	B. Notions of how much is to be covered at what rate, importance of efficiency of procedures, punctuality, correctness vs. speed, etc.
C. Values relating to purpose of education in general and relative importance of different kinds of education	C. Relative emphasis on learning an authoritative body of knowledge, on practical education, on political education, on acquiring the right credentials, on preserving the past vs. encouraging change, etc.

methods. As it now stands, the framework consists of five major categories each of which contains various related subcategories.

Cultural Values

For purposes of illustration we can consider three cultural values in an attempt to show how they bear on consideration of teaching methods and classroom practices. For a thorough, systematic investigation of differences in cultural values it is helpful to check value inventories such as the one in Condon and Yousef's *An Introduction to Intercultural Communication* (1975).

1. **Individualism/Group Orientation.** Cross-cultural variation in individualism vs. group orientation is one of the most frequently discussed value differences. The United States is regarded as a society in which the individual is paramount while the orientation in many cultures is toward the group. To fit in harmoniously with one's social group may be a dominant goal reflected in the daily patterns of life in some cultures, and to avoid losing face or being shamed vis-a-vis group members is of utmost importance in many societies. In exploring how broader cultural differences in individualism vs. group orientation are evidenced in the culture of the classroom, we must be very careful, because each value operates differently in different cultures and is manipulated in various ways in the educational setting. We cannot, for

example, conclude that a strong sense of competition does not exist in group-oriented cultures. In Japan, a highly group-directed society, places at the leading universities are fiercely competed for. However, as Shimahara (1978) points out, fueling the individual competition for university admission is the intense need to establish oneself within a group since the school one attends often determines the company one joins—usually a lifelong and all encompassing commitment in Japan. A different sort of dynamic underlines academic competition in the U.S. where the ultimate goal is individual success and where one's affiliation with social and work groups may be much more transitory and less binding than in Japan. Furthermore, while the Japanese student may need to be highly competitive with his peers for opportunities in higher education, competition in the classroom itself is not realized in the same way as in U.S. schools. Indeed, many Asian students report embarrassment at being singled out for attention or praise by teachers.

Similarly, studies of various groups of American Indian children (e.g. Philips 1972; Cazden and John 1971) who come from more group-directed cultures indicate that students may enthusiastically compete against one another in teams or work groups but are hesitant to compete overtly on an individual basis or to speak out in front of the entire class.

The strong tendency toward individual competition in U.S. education is related to another phenomenon often noticed by foreign students. In this country there is a greater sense of privacy and individual ownership about one's work and achievement. Many students from other cultures report that there is more openness about sharing of information in their countries. One fellow teacher commented to me that in Korea a student once apologized for not handing in his work because he had to write a report for a friend. Our standards of cheating and plagiarism are culture bound, and the implications for our students—especially those headed for academic work at an American institution—are clear. It must be made very explicit what constitutes cheating and plagiarism, and procedures for citing another's work, listing references, etc., must be taught thoroughly.

Another pedagogical implication of cultural differences in individualism and group orientation is that members of many strongly group-oriented cultures tend to keenly feel shame or ridicule vis-a-vis the group. Classroom practices leading to undeserved loss of face for students are going to be humiliating and most likely counterproductive. Some of the newer FL methodologies are radically different from those our students are used to, and individuals who have difficulty with them or fail to learn from them may experience a strong sense of shame and loss of face. An important point here is that methods based on group dynamics are not necessarily appropriate for students from strong group-directed cultures, and we must keep in mind that students from many of these cultures are used to much more traditional methods. Further, because of the very nature of the methods, students are more intensely involved with the group and, therefore, risk greater loss of face in failing.

2. **Time.** Considering subcategory B, attitudes toward use of time, ever since Hall's publication of *The Silent Language* (1966), we have been more aware of culturally conditioned concepts of time and attitudes toward its use. The United States is generally characterized as a fast-paced culture emphasizing efficiency, speed, and punctuality, and we might expect to see these features contrasting sharply in the classroom with characteristics of cultures having different views toward time and its use. Many intensive English students in this country remark on the extreme difficulties they experience with timed exercises and tests and make the common observation that people here always seem to be in a hurry. On the other hand, the informants interviewed for this research claim that in their countries there is heavy pressure to cover a certain amount of material in a specified sequence of time, and many state that because of the prevalence of more deductive, lecture-type methods than in the U.S., material is covered at a faster rate in their home countries, a phenomenon also noted by Grove (1977) in his study of the cross-cultural problems of Portuguese immigrant students. Quite possibly because of the requirements inherent in the educational domain we may not find as many intercultural differences in use of time inside the classroom than outside in the broader culture. However, many of our students do need training and practice in doing timed tests and exercises.

3. **Aims of Education.** Considering subcategory C, we find that different cultures value different kinds of education for different reasons. In Vietnam there is a strong veneration of book learning, for example, and several colleagues from certain Asian countries have reported that their education tends to be more theoretical than practical although this seems to be changing. Saville-Troike (1976) notes that in some cultures preservation of the existing culture is an important aim of education whereas in other societies the educational process encourages change. In places where there is a shortage of qualified personnel or where getting a good job depends primarily on merely having a credential and from there knowing the right people or belonging to the right political party, motivation to come to class regularly and study hard may be lower than in cultures where jobs are allocated on the basis of accomplishments in school.

Since the perceived purpose of education affects what material is presented, how it is learned, and the degree and type of student motivation, it is crucial for us to know if there are strong cultural differences between our students' and our own conceptions of the purpose of education and the value of different kinds of learning.

Views Toward the Teacher

The second major category to be considered is that of views toward the teacher (Table 2). Those who have studied or taught in more than one culture are often struck by the strong differences in attitudes surrounding the teacher

Table 2
Views Toward the Teacher

General Culture	Culture of the Classroom
Differences in:	Differences in:
A. Views on status, prestige of teacher; norms of appropriate distance between student and teacher	A. Rules of deference, propriety; degree of formality or informality between student and teacher
B. Views on rights and obligations of teachers, i.e., teacher role	B. 1. Degree of authority invested in and expected from teacher
	2. Degree to which teacher directs, dominates classroom activities
	3. Expectation of teacher as scholar, sage
	4. Expectation of teacher as counselor, adviser
	5. Expectation of teacher as personal tutor

and are surprised at the extent to which culturally conditioned ideas about the teacher role are reflected in norms of classroom behavior.

1. **Social Distance Between Teacher and Student.** Considering subcategory A, classroom subcultures may vary widely in their norms for verbal and nonverbal demonstration of deference and formality and, thereby, reflect broader cultural views on the degree of status and prestige due the teacher and the appropriate social distance to be maintained between student and teacher. In societies where teachers have traditionally been guardians of a sacred body of knowledge they tend to be treated with greater formality and distance. Many Arab and Asian students reveal their surprise at the informal ways both American students and teachers dress and sit in the classroom, and nearly all students from other cultures are puzzled by the generally casual manner in which American students approach and speak to their teachers.

2. **Teacher Roles.** However, in terms of implications for our language teaching methods, the most important category here has to do with cultural differences in views on the rights and obligations of the teacher, subcategory B. In many cultures the teacher exercises greater authority and plays a highly directive role in determining and controlling what goes on in the classroom. Japanese and Korean students are less likely to challenge or even question the teacher, although this may be changing somewhat with the younger generation. Egyptians have told me that the teacher in the classroom fills the role of the father or mother in the family, and therefore students hesitate to challenge his or her authority overtly.

In at least some Latin American countries, on the other hand, students are free to question the teacher, to dispute the relevance of what is being taught, and to challenge the way instruction is being handled. A number of Latin Americans have mentioned to me that students there are more expressive in the classroom and that they are surprised at what they see as the apathy and docility of their peers in the United States.

As for subcategories B-3, 4, and 5, we predictably find cultural variation in the types of duties teachers are expected to perform and the abilities they are supposed to have. In some societies there is a greater sense of teacher as scholar or sage, as one who knows a great deal and is highly respected for his knowledge. The expectation of teacher as personal adviser varies, too. A colleague who taught at a boarding school in West Africa reported that she was frequently expected to help students with personal problems. In Thailand and Japan, there is a much greater tendency for students to have a favorite professor or two to whom they will return for help and guidance, even many years after graduation. In this country, some personal tutoring is expected of teachers; that is, teachers have a responsibility for giving students individual attention and extra help. The degree to which this is expected from teachers varies across cultures.

An examination of these differences in teacher roles is an enlightening undertaking, for much of the miscommunication that occurs in the classroom may come from different expectations regarding the teacher's rights and obligations. I got very upset on one occasion with a group of Latin American students for challenging my teaching methods and on another with a former Taiwanese pupil who returned to visit me and expected an immediate and time-consuming favor even though I was no longer his teacher. My anger and frustration would have been spared if I had been aware of two of the cultural patterns that I have just described.

But what are some of the broader implications of cultural differences in the role of the teacher for our consideration of teaching methods? In considering any method or classroom procedure we have to keep in mind that students from societies where there is a high degree of teacher authority and direction may have a low tolerance for ambiguity and difficulty with activities requiring student choice and initiative. Participating in group projects and problem-solving activities and choosing a topic for and writing one's own research paper may be very difficult for students from societies where schooling is primarily a matter of "receiving" knowledge that a teacher dispenses. Students need to understand the purpose of such activities and be given concrete guidelines and support in executing them.

Brown (1977), in expressing reservations about Community Language Learning (CLL), notes that some students may need more assertive, directive behaviors than are provided for in CLL, and this may be especially true for students from cultures where the teacher is the locus of instruction. Brown also notes the excessive and varied demands made on the teacher who uses this method, and his point has special significance when we consider cultural variation in student expectations of the instructor. In a CLL session, the language material comes from the students and the teacher is expected to

Table 3
Modes of Learning

Culture of the Classroom

Differences in relative emphasis on:

- A. Inductive/deductive reasoning
- B. Learning by doing/observation before doing
- C. Discovery learning/receptive learning
- D. 1. Rote learning, memorization of facts
  - 2. Problem solving
  - 3. Creative thinking
  - 4. Critical evaluation

explain any grammar points that arise in class. There are few teachers knowledgeable enough to deliver clear, accurate, and thorough grammar explanations without advance preparation. For students from a culture where wisdom and thorough knowledge of the subject matter are an even greater expectation of the instructor, faulty explanations may not only give rise to errors in performance but also seriously undermine teacher credibility and otherwise interfere with instruction.

Modes of Learning

Proceeding to the third category, Modes of Learning (Table 3), Hall (1966) has pointed out that people learn to learn differently, and it is important to consider cultural differences in relative emphases placed on various learning strategies. For example, those used to more deductive grammar translation methods may have problems with more inductive audiolingual approaches. Considering subcategory B, some of the studies on the American Indian student have revealed striking differences in the area of learning by doing, and these hold for certain other cultures as well. Philips (1972) notes that in the home setting many Warm Springs Indian children have the opportunity to observe first and then test their skills privately before publicly trying them out. In societies where there is greater prevalence of lecture methods, students are not so often put on the spot to perform in front of their peers with little prior preparation. In contrast to this, the anthropologist Jules Henry (1976) refers to the American phenomenon of "jamming the machine," of forcing children to *do*, to *perform* very early in the learning process, possibly before they are ready. Many of our instructional techniques and language teaching methods reflect this tendency. Some varieties of pattern practice, for instance, have students using the pattern prior to much explanation of it. Techniques characteristic of a wide variety of methods emphasize student performance at an early stage of instruction, and as teachers we should be aware of minimizing the anxiety-arousing effects on some students by giving clear directions and ample models and examples.

Regarding subcategory D, a well-attested-to and frequently decried phenomenon in many cultures is the emphasis on rote learning and memorization. Smith (1977), for example, notes the emphasis on learning grammar rules and exceptions in many Asian countries. It may be difficult for these students to shift their energy from memorizing facts to gaining functional mastery over patterns through practice. For students from cultures where the process of education is seen largely as learning a traditional, authoritative body of knowledge or where factors such as class size make problem-solving and creative-thinking activities impossible, it is important once again to provide clear guidance and orientation. Furthermore, it should be kept in mind that preferred problem-solving strategies, notions of creativity, and the bases for critical evaluation may differ from one culture to another.

It may also be helpful to draw more on our students' preferred modes of learning to help them through language material, especially at the beginning stages of instruction. Students who come from strong rote-learning cultures may benefit from a lot of copying work, for example.

Teacher-Student Interaction Patterns

Included in the fourth category (Table 4) are types of student/teacher interaction patterns. The patterns of interaction that characterize a class are partly related to cultural features such as preferred modes of learning and attitudes toward the teacher. They also derive from language teaching goals and methods and are closely connected to factors such as class size, time allotted to instruction, and teacher proficiency in the target language. Thus, differences in these features of instruction are usually associated with different types of classroom interaction patterns and, especially, differences in the nature and amount of language performance expected of the student. The communicative activities which have become such a prominent aspect of language teaching in some countries may be thoroughly unfamiliar to students from systems emphasizing rule learning, translation, and reading aloud, and to students from settings where large classes, limited resources, and teachers' low proficiency in English preclude implementation of a more communicative approach to language teaching. It is important to understand that many students have never before taken part in a role play, a group problem-solving task, a story retelling exercise, or a class discussion, and that such activities entail social as well as linguistic challenges for them. Teachers can demonstrate their sensitivity to the difficulties faced by students encountering these tasks for the first time by providing careful preparation, including clear instructions and ample models, and by using the sorts of techniques that good teachers generally do, such as calling on less shy, more self-confident students first, or having more self-conscious students participate initially in smaller ways, for example, assigning them minor roles in role plays.

23

Table 4
Teacher-Student Interaction Patterns

Culture of the Classroom

Differences in preferred teacher–student interaction patterns

A. Teacher lectures, recites; students take notes, copy

B. Teacher questions students
   1. individuals called on
   2. individuals volunteer

C. Students ask questions

D. Students recite, read

E. Drill
   1. Choral
   2. Individual

F. Class discussion—students discuss or debate an issue

G. Group work
   1. Teacher works with group
   2. Group works on its own to resolve a problem, prepare a presentation, etc.

H. Peer teaching

I. Students dramatize, role play material

J. Individual work
   1. Self-paced instruction, programmed learning, etc.
   2. Student merely works by himself

K. Student gives report, speech

Among the communicative activities which have become popular in recent years are tasks which involve the students in group work for the purpose of solving a problem, preparing a report, or considering information in order to reach a decision. Some of our students from Japan have reported to their teachers that group tasks can be quite painful for them because of their uncertainty about strategies in English for reaching group consensus—a process which is highly valued in Japanese society. Watanabe (1984) suggests that group work is facilitated for Japanese students when the teacher appoints a group leader, since it is difficult for an individual to accept such a role as a result of peer discussion. On the other hand, Philips' (1972) research with Warm Springs Indian children reveals that these students participate more in self-run student groups than when the teacher is dominating the class in more typical Anglo style.

It is not only innovative activities which may cause interaction difficulties rooted in cross-cultural differences, but more traditional features of instruction as well. Some students who come from cultures where they are quite passive in the classroom find it tremendously difficult to speak unless called on by the teacher. Instructors must be careful not to overlook students who do not initiate participation.

Many students have not had any experience with individualized or self-paced instruction and find it frustrating not to be doing what the people seated around them are doing. When using such instruction, say in reading and writing classes, it may be helpful to explain carefully the principles and procedures underlying it.

Today's EFL/ESL teachers have at their disposal a large array of techniques and activities to promote accuracy and fluency in the target language, but it is important to remember that the tasks required of learners may give rise to interaction patterns which are unfamiliar and sometimes uncomfortable and that the requirements for self-expression are often much greater than students have experienced at home.

Norms of Interaction

Since the work of Hymes (1972) and other sociolinguists in the area of communicative competence we have become more aware of the ways in which our students' behavior is regulated by largely unconscious and extremely complex social interaction rules. In this framework, I note several areas (Table 5) where communicative competence rules regulate interaction in the general culture and designate the particular parallel for the classroom.

Since it is impossible to explore each category in depth, I will just mention how a few differences in social interaction rules have a bearing on classroom practice.

Norms regarding the sorts of topics considered appropriate for discussion and the amount and type of information to be disclosed (subcategories C and D) are culture-specific and may also be influenced by political factors. What seems to the teacher a simple request for factual information may be viewed as threatening or inappropriate by Middle Eastern students, who, as Parker (1976) notes, may be more willing to provide opinions than facts in certain situations. Anxiety can easily be provoked when political or social views are sought by means of seemingly harmless questions meant to elicit speech, such as "Describe the leader of your country" or "What is an important social issue in your country?" And while many students may be able to engage in frank discussion of issues such as birth control in an advanced speaking class of both males and females, others may find it embarrassing. Interesting topics need not be avoided, of course. Instead, at the beginning of the term, the teacher might send around a list of potential subjects for discussion, ask students to rank them for preference, and indicate any topics they would strongly prefer not to use.

For students going on to academic work, the English classroom provides a place in which to learn the conventions of classroom interaction, and the teacher, no matter what methods are used, should take advantage of oppor-

Table 5
Norms of Interaction
(Communicative Competence Rules)

General Culture	Culture of the Classroom
Differences in general communicative competence rules in the following areas:	Differences in classroom communicative competence rules in the following areas:
A. Address forms	A. How students/teachers address one another
B. Silence/participation	B. How much silence/participation are valued and under what conditions they should occur
C. Topics appropriate for discussion	C. What kinds of topics can be discussed in class or written about in compositions
D. Degree of self-disclosure	D. What kinds of and how much factual information and personal opinion it is appropriate for students and teachers to reveal
E. Getting attention, taking speaking turns, interrupting, etc.	E. How teachers get students' attention and vice versa, how speaking turns are taken, who interrupts whom and how, etc.
F. Proxemic patterns: use of space	F. How seating is arranged, what appropriate distances between student and teacher are
G. Kinesic patterns: body postures, gestures, and facial expressions	G. What appropriate postures, gestures, and expressions for teachers and students are and what they mean
H. Eye-contact patterns	H. What eye-contact patterns are used and what they signal
I. Touching patterns	I. What kinds of touching behaviors are appropriate for students and teachers
J. Paralinguistic patterns	J. What various paralinguistic forms and meanings are
K. Speech acts: greeting, leave taking, introductions, showing approval, showing disapproval, etc.	K. What norms underlie various classroom speech acts such as greeting the students, starting the class, dismissing the class, making introductions, praising or reprimanding students, etc.

tunities to explicitly teach customary classroom behavior, such as getting the teacher's attention and speaking in turn (subcategory E). For example, many students need to be taught not to call out "Teacher," but to simply raise their hands when they want to be called on. In many cultures, a student arriving late to class must apologize upon entering the classroom, a behavior which is considered intrusive in this country.

Foreign language teaching methods make use of a wide variety of nonverbal expressions (subcategory G), and it is important to remember that pointing is considered impolite in many cultures, as is the typical American beckoning gesture to call students to the front of the room. (In some places, it is used only for animals.) We need to be aware of the interpretations students may be attributing to certain gestures and to understand that failure to respond to certain nonverbal cues may mean that the students have not understood them.

Rules underlying the formulation and interpretation of speech acts appropriate to the classroom also vary from one culture to another. Teachers need to be especially careful about reprimands. A comment perceived as mildly sarcastic and slightly embarrassing to an American student talking to a friend in class might evoke profound embarrassment and loss of face in students from other cultures. Even praise must be handled carefully, since for students from some Asian countries it is embarrassing to stand out from one's peers, even in a positive fashion.

Complaints are also handled differently in different cultures. In the intensive program at the University of Pittsburgh in which I teach, there is at least one incident a year in which teachers become upset about students, often from countries in Latin America, going to the director to complain about their teaching. It is not the students' dissatisfaction which bothers the teachers so much, but the fact that the students go over their heads rather than attempting to first resolve the problem with them.

There is much more which could be said about cultural differences in classroom interaction rules. Further research will enable us to understand such differences better and provide the information necessary to teach our students the norms appropriate to their academic experiences in this country.

In conclusion, I think it is necessary to address the issue of where to find the information that will allow us to examine systematically aspects of our teaching methods and classroom practices according to the sort of framework suggested here. Springer (1977) deplores the lack of comparative work in pedagogy and classroom practice, and until this problem is remedied, we must depend on other resources. But the situation is far from bleak. Within the fields of sociolinguistics, anthropology, educational anthropology, applied linguistics, and intercultural communication, there are many sources from which we can extract cross-cultural information that is readily applied to the classroom. Indeed, with the growing concern with linguistic and cultural issues surrounding ethnic minority children, foreign students, and our adult immigrants, we find an increasing amount of information directly relevant to instruction in the ESL/EFL classroom.

Of course, the multicultural classroom itself provides a wealth of information to the inquiring, sensitive observer. Many of us can draw on our experience and that of our colleagues, both in the United States and abroad, in reaching conclusions about cultural differences in the classroom. As Paulston (1975) points out, our students can be effectively used as informants of their own cultures, and this requires us as teachers to behave as amateur anthropologists. A crucial part of the process is knowing what questions to ask. A framework of the sort offered here provides a guideline in the process of exploring cultural differences as they apply to teaching methods and classroom practices. It is a first approximation, and my hope is that further thinking and more empirical research will provide additional categories and furnish a basis for a sound, workable model for the cross-cultural analysis of foreign language teaching methods and classroom practices.

BACKGROUND DISCUSSIONS

Toward a Model for Cross-Cultural Orientation

GREGORY A. BARNES
Drexel University

A goal which unites all those who deal with the community of international students and scholars is the acculturation of their clientele. It has not always been this way; at one time, those of us who teach English as a second language saw acculturation as other people's work, or as little more than a natural concomitant of our own. The rise of sociolinguistics during the past two decades has altered this perception and, indeed, has led some (e.g. Schumann 1978) to claim that there is a correlation between language-learning and acculturation, if not an equation.

As a result, we increasingly incorporate cultural materials in language training, or are urged to do so (Hughes 1984). We also attempt to hasten the process of adjustment through a variety of extracurricular events which we usually fit under the rubric, "cross-cultural orientation." But what, in fact, is cross-cultural orientation, and how does it or should it operate? This paper examines a wide variety of orientation events and suggests three criteria— contact, relevance, and structuring potential—by which they may be evaluated.

Current Conceptions of Cross-Cultural Orientation

It is not always clear from the literature on cross-cultural orientation just what, exactly, such orientation is or accomplishes. One problem lies in the use of overlapping terms applied to similar activities. Thus, Smith and Luce (1979) speak of cross-cultural "communication"; Althen *et al.* (1981) write of "intercultural educational activity"; Pusch (1979) has titled her book *Multicultural Education: A Cross Cultural Training Approach*; and the terms "trans-cultural" and "bicultural" appear here and there. Moreover, the term "cross-cultural"—implying as it does the give and take of values between

29

cultures—covers orientations which are essentially "cultural," in that they transmit the values of the host society to the sojourner. Brislin and Pedersen (1976:1) offer an apposite definition: "Cross-cultural orientation programs are designed to teach members of one culture ways of interacting effectively, with minimal interpersonal misunderstanding, in another culture."

Those writers who have dealt at length with the general concept of cross-cultural orientation address principally its importance and various activities they consider useful. The latter include highly structured training courses whose objective is overtly (not implicitly) intercultural understanding, best seen in Hoopes and Ventura (1979), as well as ESL classes such as those devoted to "intercultural conversation," proposed by Dunnett (1981:58). More commonly, orientations are seen as extracurricular activities whose ostensible purpose is information-sharing or conviviality rather than acculturation. Thus, Foust *et al.* (1981) recommend a range of activities which include practical (or "survival") information sessions, homestays, international club events, and culture-specific seminars.

Such extracurricular activities are the focus of this paper. For the purposes of my study, I separate the idea of cross-cultural orientation from ESL training *per se*, thus excluding such activities as Dunnett's conversation classes or the classroom roleplay suggested by Donahue and Parsons (1982). Moreover, I start from the definition of Brislin and Pedersen and apply the term to those activities which help foreign students adjust to American life—that is, to *cultural* orientations. Operating within these parameters, I will attempt to define patterns in such orientations which lead to success or failure.

Background to the Study

The data for this study come from the experiences in the Program in Teacher Preparation for Foreign Graduate Assistants at Drexel University, which I have directed since its inception in 1981. The program consists of six weeks of intensive English language review, teacher training, and cultural activities held prior to the start of the academic year. Between 20 and 25 foreign graduate students participate annually; they are divided into two streams for English and teacher training but come together for most of the cross-cultural events.

From the beginning in 1981, cross-cultural activities have been accorded large blocks of time in the program. Figure 1 shows the dimensions of the cross-cultural component: In addition to pre- and post-training social events, three or four afternoons per week are devoted to events aimed at orienting the trainees to their new campus and urban environments and to American life generally. Each Friday, the participants evaluate the events of that week. At program's end, they are asked, in the course of exit interviews, to comment further on the cross-cultural component.

The basis for determining the worth of a cross-cultural activity—and the criterion I use in what follows—has been the trainees' response, measured in

Figure 1
Configuration of Academic and Cross-Cultural Events
Program in Teacher Preparation for Foreign Graduate Assistants

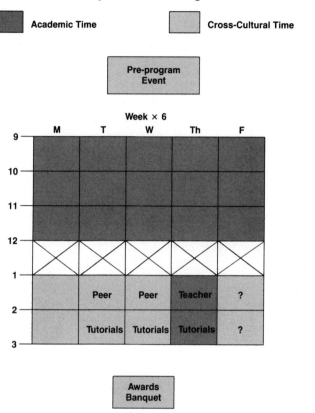

Academic Time   **Cross-Cultural Time**

Pre-program Event

Week × 6

Awards Banquet

two ways: by the trainees' actual participation in the event, and by their evaluation of it. Participation is obligatory for all but the few second-year students who request to join the program (and who usually have courses or research to see to in the afternoons). "Required attendance" is an unfamiliar concept, however, to new foreign students who often fail to appear; in their absence they have provided us a little cross-cultural education of our own, as well as insights into the worth of our events.

Based on these two measures, the degree of success or failure can be established for each event. It should be noted that financial constraints, the needs of the academic program, and scheduling problems have rarely been factors in structuring the cross-cultural component, which runs, so to speak, on a free-market basis: if an activity works, we have found the time and money to schedule it. Thus, a review of our four years of activities provides a

31

reasonably large sample of cross-cultural events which can be judged on their own terms.

The Data

Table 1 provides a complete listing of orientation events scheduled annually for this program since 1981. The number of repetitions does not, of course, indicate the degree of success (although an unrepeated event usually implies failure). A nutrition lecture inaugurated in 1981 has been reasonably well received and is, therefore, repeated annually. Peer tutorials—devoted to cultural, not linguistic, topics—are more successful but more recent.

From the attendance figures and participant comments, three categories of events may be established for analysis: "Real" Successes (well attended, highly rated events), Modest Successes (events which were reasonably well attended and not unfavorably evaluated), and Failures. Capsule summaries of representative events are shown in Table 2, for reference in the analysis which follows.

The questions I have sought to answer are these: Did successful events share certain attributes? And did the events which failed not share these attributes? The answer is "yes," in both cases.

Analysis

Four of the events summarized in Table 2 deserve elaboration here in that they form two contrasting sets. The first has to do with a pre-program "ice-breaking" event:

In 1983, a pre-program tour of New York City was arranged, including visits to the United Nations and the Empire State Building, and a boat trip around Manhattan. The tour was conducted by two staff members and cost $500. It failed; only seven trainees showed up. In 1984, the New York trip was replaced by a picnic. Four staff members came to campus in their cars to pick up the trainees and take them to a park; two peer tutors (undergraduate students) also participated. The group broiled hamburgers and threw frisbees for two hours, then returned home. All of the trainees turned out, and they expressed considerable appreciation for the event.

The second illustrative set contrasts the campus tour and the tour of Philadelphia (see Table 2):

The tour of Philadelphia was intended to give the newcomers both a flavor of the city which was to be their home for the next few years and insights into the evolution of American society. Only four trainees came along on the tour, however, and they showed no great enthusiasm for it in the regular Friday program evaluations. The most favorable comment had a bittersweet taste: "I was touched by Dr. Barnes taking the time to give us this opportunity." The campus tour includes an extended stop at the gymnasium, where the athletic director leads the group on a tour of all the facilities available to them, and considerable time is also spent in the Main Building, where the

Table 1
Longitudinal Array of Afternoon Orientation Activities, Program in Teacher Preparation for Foreign Graduate Assistants

Time	1981	1982	1983	1984
Pre-Prog.	--- *	---	Bus trip, New York	Picnic in park
WEEK 1 — M	Campus tour	Campus tour	Campus tour	Peer tutorials
WEEK 1 — T	Nutrition talk	Library tour	Peer tutorials	Peer tutorials
WEEK 1 — W	Walking tour, Old Philadelphia	---	Peer tutorials	---
WEEK 1 — Th	International House	---	---	Campus tour
WEEK 1 — F	---	Picnic in park	---	---
WEEK 2 — M	Library tour	Library tour	Library tour	Library tour
WEEK 2 — T	Visit to bank	Tour of Philadelphia	Peer tutorials	Peer tutorials
WEEK 2 — W	Health Clinic briefing	---	---	Peer tutorials
WEEK 2 — Th	Lunch, Indian restaurant	---	---	---
WEEK 2 — F	---	---	---	International House
WEEK 3 — M	U. of Pennsylvania Museum	Foreign student adviser	Foreign student adviser	Foreign student adviser
WEEK 3 — T	Visit to Civic Center	---	Peer tutorials	Peer tutorials
WEEK 3 — W	Visit to supermarket	---	---	Peer tutorials
WEEK 3 — Th	Visit to Balch Institute	---	---	---
WEEK 3 — F	---	---	---	---

Table 1—Continued

Time		1981	1982	1983	1984
W	M	Franklin Institute	AV demonstration	AV demonstration	AV demonstration
E	T	---	Franklin Institute	Peer tutorials	Peer tutorials
E	W	---	---	Peer tutorials	Peer tutorials
K	Th	Housing orientation	---	---	---
4	F	---	---	---	---
W	M	Longwood Gardens	---	International House	---
E	T	Visit to funeral home	---	Peer tutorials	Peer tutorials
E	W	Visit to shopping center	International House	Peer tutorials	Peer tutorials
K	Th	Visit to art museum	---	---	---
5	F	---	---	Assoc. Dean, Engineering: grading policies	Assoc. Dean, Engineering: grading policies
W	M	---	Nutrition talk	---	---
E	T	Lunch, Chinese restaurant	---	---	---
E	W	Visit to zoo	---	Nutrition talk	Nutrition talk
K	Th	Industry visit	---	---	---
6	F	---	Longwood Gardens	---	---
Post-Prog.		---	---	Awards Banquet	Awards Banquet

Dashes (---) indicate either an academic event, no activity, or Labor Day holiday.

Table 2
Representative Orientation Events
Real Successes

1. **Pre-program Picnic.** Staff and family members, driving their own cars, take trainees to local park to grill hot dogs and hamburgers.
2. **Walking Tour, Campus.** Comprehensive tour of campus: colleges and other pertinent buildings pointed out, extended visits to gymnasium (tour by athletic director) and Main (administrative) Building.
3. **Peer Tutorials.** The only repeating event. Ten two-hour sessions with Drexel undergraduates on cultural/university (not ESL) topics.
4. **Meeting the Foreign Student Adviser.** Session devoted to immigration requirements and FSA services.
5. **Meeting with Associate Dean, Engineering.** A review of university grading policies, open to both engineering and non-engineering students.

Modest Successes

1. **Visit to International House.** Tour of International House by IH staff member. Introduction to IH services (apartment rentals, international events, films, etc.)
2. **Nutrition Lecture.** Faculty member, Nutrition Department, briefs trainees on nutrition needs and answers questions on finding preferred foods or substitutes.
3. **Ethnic Lunches.** Staff-escorted lunches at one Indian, one Chinese restaurant.

Failures

1. **Pre-program Trip to New York City.** All-day tour; visits to U.N., and Empire State Building, and boat trip around Manhattan. Travel to and from New York by university bus.
2. **Tour of Philadelphia.** Trolley and subway to Independence Hall, walking tour of Society Hill (Old Philadelphia), bus ride back through attractions of center city.
3. **Visit to Supermarket.** Orientation to nearby supermarket, including food sections, pricing, etc.
4. **Visit to Philadelphia Art Museum.** By public transportation. Students free to browse.
5. **Visit to Student Health Clinic.** Orientation to American medical care and insurance, and to health services available on campus.

---

trainees see offices of university administrators whom they have already met or who will soon play a part in their lives. This tour has been well attended.

These contrasting sets yield at least two patterns for consideration. In both cases, it is evident that the students chose interaction over sightseeing and getting down to business (learning about the TA program, getting a feel for the campus) over discovering America. A third pattern is at least suggested: The students chose events which helped them organize the days and weeks to come. It is from these three patterns that a model for the cross-cultural orientation event emerges.

The Model

Analysis of the data in Tables 1 and 2 suggests that the three criteria elicited from the contrasting sets above can be used to predict success or failure for an orientation event. The criteria may be stated as follows:

1. **Meaningful Contact with Americans.** An orientation event should provide students the opportunity to interact with Americans, and in such a way as to allow the students to believe they have established ongoing contacts. The contrast between city and campus tours is instructive, for on the campus tour the trainees encountered the athletic director and, glancingly, other Americans who promised to be meaningful to them. The tour of Philadelphia gave them glimpses of a larger body of Americans but people who would forever be strangers to them.

Other real successes were conspicuous for meaningful contact. The pre-program picnic, for example, gave the trainees a chance to meet the instructional staff with whom they would work intensively for six weeks. By contrast, the failures reveal an emphasis on showing and telling rather than establishing interaction. The New York trip provides a cautionary example.

2. **Immediate Relevance.** The relevance of an orientation event should be apparent to the participants. Foust *et al* (1981:12–13) have noted that "sojourners will be preoccupied with . . . immediate needs and will be unable to turn their attention to more abstract considerations of cultural adjustment until these needs are satisfied." The statement is supported by this research. In the early stages of their visit, the trainees apparently saw Philadelphia merely as a backdrop to their sojourn (and American society as an entity beyond their immediate interest). The tour of New York City lacked direct relevance, as did the visit to the Philadelphia Art Museum (Table 2).

By contrast, the registrar's and comptroller's offices had immediacy for the students, for these small entities were to impose large demands on them. The relevance of the other successes listed in Table 2 is both immediate and apparent.

3. **A Potential for Structure.** An orientation event should provide long-term applications. This third criterion emerging from the Drexel study is largely inferential, yet consistent with the data: Students newly arrived in a foreign country look for ways by which they can structure their lives—just as Americans would overseas. It is appropriate to note here the profile drawn by Lee *et al.* (1981) of the "satisfied" (adjusted) foreign student, among whose characteristics are three which imply a sense of foreseen structures: (1) a student who has a job waiting for him or her at home; (2) a student who is residing with a U.S. student; (3) a student who is on an assistantship. The second of these relates principally to the criterion of contact but also suggests a personal agenda, that of developing a *modus vivendi* with a native.

The most successful orientation efforts seemed to provide the trainees a vision of a structure for carrying out aspects of their daily lives. Thus, the campus tour offered them a feel for geography and considerations of agendas (how easy will it be to get in a swim at lunchtime? how will the registration procedure work? where will I find my new friend Arun when he is working? should I rent an apartment in or near those dormitories?). The tour of Philadelphia, like most other unsuccessful events, provided them no such visions.

Discussion

Overall, the real successes in orienting foreign teaching assistants to their new setting shared at least two of the variables defined here. Peer tutorials embodied the first two: the undergraduates serving as peers provided both meaningful contact and immediate relevance to the lives of teaching assistants, who would soon be instructing young Americans just like them. The pre-program picnic gave the trainees contact with the entire staff (including peer tutors) as well as a chance to anticipate the structure of upcoming days, through relaxed, informal conversation. The meetings with the foreign student adviser and the associate dean of engineering (on grading policies) dealt with the matters of immediate relevance and set up agendas for the trainees' immigration and academic duties respectively.

Conversely, the unsuccessful events show only one of these variables or none. The trip to New York—although it seems the event many of us would most like if we were newcomers to the United States—was lacking in all three. The unsuccessful visit to the health clinic stood the model on its head: Here were contacts the trainees wished never to be meaningful, a relevance they dared not consider immediate, and a foreseen agenda they could only view as unpleasant. As for our visit to a funeral home, nothing need be said.

Explaining the differing fates of two similar events—the trip to a supermarket and the nutrition lecture (Table 2)—is more difficult. Our visit to the supermarket should have provided both immediacy and structure (everyone has to eat and to arrange for food), but it was not successful. The nutrition lecture would seem to provide *only* structure, but has been relatively popular. This is a gray area which needs further exploration. My own inference is that the trainees envisioned themselves finding substitutes for their preferred foods, but not at a supermarket, and that their responses do not invalidate my three criteria.

Conclusions

The model arrived at may be stated as a working definition: Cross-cultural orientation is an activity which helps people of one culture adjust to another culture by providing contact with the people of the other culture, immediately relevant means of accommodating themselves to the other culture, and/or opportunities for the newcomers to foresee a structure for living within the other culture. Like most working definitions, it needs refinement. Three problem areas may be identified:

First, more variables are likely. Food and drink, widely shared symbols of fellowship, may partially account for the success of our picnic. Peer tutorials may be popular because most Drexel trainees are young men, and our tutors, young women. In addition, such events such as "culture assimilators" and critical incidents training (see Hoopes and Ventura 1979), which are not explored here, focus on the variable of conflict resolution. The extent to which these variables are signficant is a problem for further research and experimentation.

Second, the experiences of one institution are not a sufficient basis on which to form a valid model. Drexel's foreign teaching assistants work almost entirely in the sciences and engineering. It is possible that foreign students in other fields will be less interested in immediately relevant experiences, more interested in off-campus tours.

Third, a fuller means of evaluating the success of orientation in the acculturation process is needed (for a sophisticated evaluation design, see Brislin and Pedersen 1976: 159–176). The response, physical and/or verbal, of the participants is surely a valid measurement, but it is probably not totally reliable, in that such a measurement places paramount faith in newcomers' instincts at a time when they are experiencing considerable confusion.

The variables of contact, immediacy, and structuring potential nevertheless hold promise as predictors for the success or failure of an orientation event. Their validity also brings into question several activities which are often considered cross-cultural orientations. "It is difficult," write Foust et al. (1981:16), "to apply theoretical knowledge obtained through orientation, books, films or conversations to the actual process of cross-cultural adaptation." I would add that, indeed, a "theoretical" orientation in which some large topic is "explained" in a presenter-audience format lacks resonance for newcomers, and that film and text are inadequate substitutes for effective cross-cultural orientation.

These ideas go beyond the scope of the present study. I suggest, by way of conclusion, that several questions remain to be raised and answered about the phenomenon of cross-cultural orientation. The working model developed here for that phenomenon is meant as a starting point for those questions.

BACKGROUND DISCUSSIONS

Cultural Styles of Thinking and Speaking in the Classroom

KEITH MAURICE
Florida State University

Culture supplies us with fixed ways of viewing life, people, and the ways of the world. We unconsciously use it as a filter to sort through the complex web of possible meanings and interpretations that we could give to the millions of stimuli we face yearly. But the same filter that protects us from the glare of confusion also blocks us from other valid ways of viewing. As such, culture represents both a passageway to the world and a prison that keeps us from it. Cultural patterns provide us with a stable foundation from which to survive and prosper, but they also deaden our sensitivities as well. "The mental patterns of one's own group become unquestioned 'common sense' and 'human nature.' This is very functional at home; it plays havoc abroad" (Fisher 1979:110). No matter how sophisticated we become with regard to other cultures, we must constantly strive for an awareness of the cultural baggage that surrounds our perceptions.

Communication involves the exchange of meanings between people. The intent of communication is to make meanings understood in the same way by both the speaker and the listener. The fact of communication is that, regardless of the intent, we communicate something every time we interact with another human being. With a similar cultural background, the perceptions of both parties often concur. But with differing backgrounds, the perceptions more often diverge. What is intended is missed or brushed aside while what is not intended is considered the key point of the whole message.

In order to pursue cross-cultural communication effectively in the language classroom, we need to delve into the cultural assumptions, beliefs, ways of viewing, and communicative styles that may hinder understanding. Rather than ignoring the challenges that conflict presents, we need to face the conflict, analyze it, and then move toward making it into cooperation. Learning a second language can give people a key with which to enter another world; but whether the experience becomes mutually satisfying or merely a nightmare in a cultural "Twilight Zone" depends on the search for and understanding of the cultural styles of thinking and speaking that converge at the ESL center.

Learners need to know how other cultures view such matters as character and credibility, how emotions are aroused and exhibited, and how logic and perception are organized in communicative settings. We need "to identify what might be called 'rules of meaning' that distinguish one culture from another" (Barnlund 1975:9). These rules of meaning that are incorporated into styles of self-presentation are the cause of much misperception and miscommunication. One's style of thinking and the resultant style of speaking often become as important as the message itself. McLuhan's famous dictum, "The medium *is* the message," may seem a bit strong, but the implications are quite real and far-reaching. How we think and how we express what we think frequently determine whether our attempts at communication are successful in getting our intended meanings across to others.

Cultural Patterns of Thinking

Americans generally view individual freedom and independence as benchmark values of our society. Japanese, on the other hand, tend to value the group and being part of the group much more than individual freedom. The respective societies reinforce those values in many different ways. Thus, Americans exhibit their individuality in many ways, from changing jobs at will to pulling up roots and moving elsewhere. Japanese, for various reasons, tend to stick to the same company and devote much more of their time to lubricating their social environment. Ouchi (1981:33) clarifies this difference: "In the U.S. we conduct our careers between organizations but within a single specialty. In Japan people conduct careers between specialities but within a single organization." Each culture has deeply embedded sets of assumptions about what is 'good' from which its particular way of thinking is derived. As such, what may seem clearly correct and logical to an American may appear comically flawed or illogical to someone else. Complicating any attempt we make to overcome the assumptions is the fact that we do not freely choose them and, in many cases, are not fully aware of their effect on us; they are thrust upon us early in life and we must work long and hard to overcome the frailties of our filters.

Styles of Logic

Logic, on the surface, seems a fairly straightforward matter. One looks at the facts presented and then proceeds to build conclusions from the facts. But cultural values and assumptions mold what we perceive as relevant facts and irrelevant trivia. In one study of cultural styles of persuasion, which are directly related to styles of thinking, Glenn, Witmeyer, and Stevenson (1977) ana-

40

lyzed meetings of the U.N. Security Council concerning the Arab-Israeli War. They identified three general styles of presenting information:

1. *Factual-inductive*: facts are studied first and conclusions are then drawn from those facts,
2. *Axiomatic-deductive*: a general theory is first advanced and then facts are studied within that framework,
3. *Intuitive-affective*: positions are expressed through appeals and emotions.

Their findings point to very pronounced differences between cultures. American delegates used the first approach, factual-inductive, twice as much as the second and did not use the intuitive-affective mode at all. Soviet delegates, on the other hand, used the axiomatic-deductive approach five times as much as the other two approaches, while the Arab delegates were four times as likely to use the intuitive-affective approach as the others.

Where cultural styles of persuasion, and thinking, differ this much, the amount of effective communication will be greatly reduced. Each style is wrapped in a framework that demands a sharing of assumptions and values by all parties. When this sharing does not occur, the context for interaction becomes very jumbled indeed.

Another way of viewing the three styles listed above is in terms of the orientations involved. The predominant Soviet style is geared toward an idea from which everything flows; the American style is much more action-oriented; and the Arab style is more oriented toward the person. For idea-oriented thinkers, compromise is often seen as alien, but for action-oriented pragmatists, it is generally viewed as the key to getting things done (Wedge and Muromcew 1965). One group centers on a vision while the other strives for movement. The people-orientation of the Arabs pushes them in another direction. "Thought and verbal expression can be relatively uncorrelated with what circumstances actually allow" (Glenn and Glenn 1981:255). Patai states that the Arab mind contains a "psychologically conditioned substitution of words for action" (1983:65). Words thus focus on feelings and appearance rather than on an elaboration of an idea or as a source of action.

Where the style can be adapted to take into account the dominant tendencies of a particular audience, the possibilities for more effective communication increase. Wedge (1968) studied the way Brazilian students handled information about the assassination of John F. Kennedy. For the most part, the Brazilians were inclined to refute the Warren Commission's report and to accept the conspiracy theory instead. The approach used by the Americans was:

> to gather, examine, and test the evidence in laborious detail. Having concluded on the basis of facts . . . , we tried to communicate our conclusions. We failed completely with these students, for we expected them to give the same weight to the evidence as we did (Wedge 1968:32).

The facts were countered with other, sometimes far-fetched "facts," and then the Brazilians went on to argue rationally from their own theories. "Americans, in their frustration, tended to resent the Brazilians' stubborn suspicion of evidence. Brazilian students, for their part, did not find American styles of logic credible" (Wedge 1968:33). But by altering his style of presentation without changing his basic position, Wedge found more success. One approach involved confronting the conspiracy theory with another theory and then discussing the evidence in that framework. The second approach involved talking of Earl Warren as a man, building up his credibility as a fair and reasonable seeker of truth. Both were successful in overcoming the Brazilians' initial disbelief of the evidence.

The Abstract Versus the Associative

Using a different vantage point, Glenn and Glenn (1981) suggest that there are two fundamental ways that lead to commonly shared experiences. On one end of the continuum is the abstractive way, in which concepts are given ever more precise definitions so as to avoid misperception. At the other end lies the associative way in which people who share the same habits and experiences develop meanings in a non-rigorous pattern of association. American academic culture generally follows the abstractive way, while the associative way is usually found in relatively small communities or in large, traditional societies or those exposed to charismatic experiences. Most Arab societies fit into the second mode. In those societies, "the most important role of speech within the culture is to provide the participants with a mechanism for the sharing of affect" (Glenn and Glenn 1981:261).

A case that took place in the United Nations illustrates the complexity involved when differing sets of thinking interact. American and Soviet experts gave advice to Third World diplomats on a housing problem. While the Soviets strongly advocated an approach they had previously used successfully in the U.S.S.R., the American called for more caution, stating that each case had to be evaluated before any specific solutions could be successfully implemented. Though the American's position seems quite reasonable, the majority of the Third World diplomats considered:

> the Soviet point of view as being friendly toward them, and the American point of view as being inimical. (One stated that) "The Russians want us to adopt the solution which has worked for them; this means that they consider us as brothers. The Americans say that what they do themselves may not be applicable to us; this means that they look at us with contempt." (Glenn and Glenn 1981:287)

The intent of the American was to give the best advice possible; the perceived content of the American's message was a display of arrogance and apathy toward their problems. The American looked at the situation as a problem to be investigated, while the Russian already had a solution in mind. The people from the Third World responded in terms of who showed a sense of common experience with them. Quite clearly, it is not enough in such cases to look at the problem at hand; we must also look at our audience and try to gauge how they perceive both the issue and the interaction.

This brings up the whole matter of expertise and trustworthiness. In much of the developing world, trustworthiness is seen as more important than expertise, while that is often reversed in the Western world. The American above was possibly more knowledgeable than the Soviet on the complexities of housing, but was naive in assuming that the audience would appreciate that as much as Americans do. For many foreign people in an American setting, the reverse may also be true; people readily show their good character only to find that Americans downgrade it while wanting something else in its place.

Implications

"The tricky task is to gain an objective perspective. How can one place oneself emotionally and intellectually outside the entire international communication system to make impartial judgements?" (Fisher 1979:11). Such a task may be impossible, but attempts must be made to strategically replace our cultural filters with the filter of one who tries to bridge the differences in ways of viewing. As the last U.N. example has shown, people attribute motives to the words and actions of others based on their own cultural norms and values. But those attributions are too often in error. In intensive English programs, it is very easy for teachers and administrators to look at the stated goals of the students and then to develop programs geared to those narrowly defined goals, with the resulting alienation and withdrawal of some of the students and the confusion and apathy of others. Our task is not simply to become objective in the American sense, but to become as fully aware as we can of the twin contexts of culture and communication.

Students and teachers alike need to be able to anticipate culturally divergent styles of thinking and to develop cross-culturally appropriate ways of handling the troublesome situations that inevitably arise. If, for instance, two students from an Arab culture take part in a program and one is held back while the other is promoted, we can generally anticipate that some kind of protest will be forthcoming. In such situations, it is not enough for administrators to explain rationally the test scores and the program's policies. That may satisfy an American, but probably not the Arab who has been held back. A strategy needs to be developed in which the administrator, and perhaps the teachers as well, can show emotional support and a sense of emphaty with the student while still adhering to "logical" criteria for dealing with the matter.

Students need to be instructed in the differing ways of thinking; they also need to be given chances to realize the ramifications of not adhering to American standards *before* the crunch of failing hits them. Case studies, simulations, and general discussions in class can be used effectively for those purposes. All parties involved need to take extra steps early on and then repeatedly down the road to ensure a somewhat more smoothly running system. Too often ESL professionals brief students on American ways and then proceed to deal with them as we would deal with other Americans. But our students need more than just a briefing, and we need more as well. We operate in a cross-cultural context and are at the forefront of providing links to understanding between cultures. The conflicts we face will never go away completely, but if we use our opportunities well, we can turn the conflict into mutually satisfying growth experiences and heightened awareness of ourselves and of others.

Cultural Patterns of Speaking Language

"Language is as it is because of what it has to do" (Halliday 1978:19). That is to say, we cannot look at language without also looking at the functions it must perform; we cannot merely view it in the abstract, but must also view it in terms of how it is actually used. As Grimshaw has noted, "observers of human social behavior see that behavior as persistent, patterned, non-random, and rule-governed" (1981:204). If human behavior can be characterized by habitual actions, which are heavily influenced by cultural patterns, we might also expect that the language used in that behavior would also contain some habitual elements. Recent research suggests that this is the case (Coulmas 1981; Grice 1975; Richards 1980; Yorio 1980).

Language in the abstract may be a vast and only partially charted wilderness, but language in society is not. Although we have the capacity to create completely novel utterances forever, the reality of human existence molds us into using routines and ritualized ways of communicating far more than we would like to think. In the greetings we use, the compliments and apologies we give, the stories we tell, and the opinions we state, what is often striking is the repetitiveness of the words and phrases used. Our well-worn phrases help to domesticate the linguistic wilderness. Routinized language enables us to create a foundation of understanding between speaker and listener, to comfort one another, and to prepare each other for the communication to follow.

Culture in Conversation

Because each culture places emphasis on different types of communicative skills and strategies, those concerned with language need to look at culture's role in conversation as a crucial component of the total picture. Once people become accustomed to the ways their culture handles communicative interaction, they also become entrenched in the habits and cloak them with "natural" and even "moral" overtones. The whole area of intercultural communication then becomes a scene of ever-present challenges to one's deepest-felt sense of identity. As Coulmas states, "conversational routines are tacit agreements which the members of a community presume to be shared by every reasonable co-member" (1981:4). Thus, a departure from the accepted rou-

44

tines of any speech community may result in the speaker being perceived as unreasonable, undesirable, or abnormal.

Culture's role in conversation takes many forms. Conventionalized language is used quite distinctly and with various levels of frequency from culture to culture. How language is used to express directness in communication also differs greatly. Aggressiveness in conversation is very much a culture-bound characteristic as well. Culture's pervasive influence in language use extends into many areas, but these three will be briefly outlined below.

1. **Routines.** In the U.S., heavy use of conventionalized language sometimes signals a lack of intelligence or sincerity, even though we make frequent use of it. However, in some cultures, notably that of the Japanese, such stigma is not attached to conversational conventions. What is important is to say the right thing at the right time. "Linguistic etiquette requires the speaker to make extensive use of routines, often leaving little room for variation" (Coulmas 1981:90).

2. **Directness.** Americans often open conversations with comments about the weather, but Loveday (1982) notes that some German observers regard such behavior as mentally deficient. Whether a situation calls for a complaint or request or some other way of dealing with conflict, Germans tend to be more direct and to the point than Americans. In citing differences between Lithuanians and Americans, Drazdauskiene reports that:

English is verbally more courteous and less straightforward than Lithuanian. It is mainly because of the neglect of this feature in learning English as a foreign language that some Lithuanian speakers of English are said to sound rude to native speakers of English (1981:60-61).

Japanese, on the other hand, emphasizes indirectness to a much greater extent than American English. Elaborate care is taken *not* to be straightforward when communicating.

3. **Aggressiveness.** This feature, which is related to but distinct from directness, also varies a great deal from culture to culture. French and German speakers seem to use an argumentative type of discussion where the goal is "not just to ventilate ideas, but to clarify controversial points as they come up" (Kramsch 1981a:19). The American style is more akin to an informal debate, with somewhat fewer interruptions exhibited. But, regardless of whether the style is one of argument or of informal debate, Japanese sometimes see the behavior as insincere and the conversation as an artificial game. As Loveday notes, they "prefer to stress mutuality and the emotive in social interaction. 'No' almost constitutes a term of abuse" (1982:68). These represent three quite different ways of conversing, and there are many other variations among peoples who must converse a great deal with one another. It is often at this intersection of language and culture that communication fails.

Conversation

"The process of conversation displays a continual tension between two general communicative needs—the need to communicate as efficiently as possible and the need to be polite" (Laver 1981:290). Efficient communication is not always the highest priority. Politeness concerns, defined by each culture, become imposed on the communicative act. With that influence, a whole set of conventions, routines, formulae, and conversational strategies become an important and indispensable part of the language. The *how* of our speech can thus become as important as the *what*. Hence a seeming paradox exists: *Efficient communication is often ineffective while effective communication is often inefficient.*

Conversation has a structure apart from the words spoken. The rules are ritualized to some extent and yet remain flexible, leaving them slippery to analyze. Conversational structure relates to such matters as taking and holding the floor, continuing and expanding previous points, digressing, taking leave, and so on. Knowing the appropriate structure allows the listener to become comfortable with the whole context of the interaction. Without understanding this structure, the speaker will be doomed to offend and be offended by those who follow the rules of a different structure.

Conversational Management Strategies

In our interactions with others, we use various strategies, both consciously and unconsciously, to guide the interaction in ways pleasing to us. In conversations, these strategies are used often; from rather standardized and specialized formulae, such as "It's nice to see you" to more complicated signals, such as "by the way" or "what I meant to say," these strategies inundate our speaking patterns. Names given to such strategies range from conventions to routines to prefabricated phrases and formulae to gambits. For the sake of simplicity, this article will focus on what Kramsch (1981a) has called conversational management strategies, also called gambits by Keller (1980a) and Beneke (1981). Generally speaking, the simpler conventions are used in rather obvious situations and are recognized for their automaticity. Conversational management strategies, on the other hand, are less obvious and more complicated. A particular strategy can be used to push a conversation in one direction, or not used, which will push the conversation in another direction. So, although there is structuring, there is also ambiguity as to which strategies will be used in any specific conversation.

These strategies are used to move the ongoing game of conversation along. What makes them interesting to language educators is that "they are habitually used and perceived but rarely consciously noted and almost never talked about directly" (Gumperz 1982:131). Where second language learners have difficulties in this arena, they will feel uncomfortable and yet probably not know why or what they can do to solve the problem. As Beneke has observed, these strategies:

are phrases used mainly for the regulation of social relationships and the structuring of discourse. They "take the edge off" what is being said, "soften the blow" of critical remarks, or "lubricate" the conversation. A typical example . . .is to say "You may have a point there, but . . ." instead of "You are wrong" or even "Rubbish!" (1981:82-83)

Mistakes in this kind of game cause the speaker and listener to lose precious opportunities to come to common understanding. Perhaps even more important is that these mistake-ridden interactions can damage cross-cultural relationships when they are most vulnerable, i.e., when people are just beginning to get to know each other.

Conversation is a temporary partnership in which the precise roles of each partner are negotiated throughout the interaction. Conversational management strategies are the tools with which we can smoothly guide and influence that communicative negotiation. A few types of strategies, along with examples, are as follows:

1. Announcing/taking the floor: "Did you hear about. . . ."
2. Redirecting the conversation: "By the way" or "Anyway"
3. Hesitating: "Well," "You know," or "Let me see"
4. Interrupting: "Excuse me" or "Hold it a minute"
5. Retaking the floor: "What I meant to say is . . ."
6. Rephrasing: "In other words" or "What you're saying is . . ."
7. Generalizing: "On the whole" and "All things considered"
8. Persuading: "Wouldn't you agree" and "Don't you think. . . ."
9. Disagreeing: from "Not necessarily" to "On the contrary"
10. Piggy-backing: "And another thing" or "And what's more"
11. Ending discussion on a topic: "Well, all I can say is . . ."
12. Closing a conversation: "Well, I'll let you go now"

(See the Keller and Warner series, 1976-1979, for a much more complete listing.) Those who can use these strategies well can succeed in communicating smoothly and effectively, but those who ignore or use them badly will find themselves stumbling painfully, or blindly alienating their partners, while failing to communicate their true intent.

Each strategy can serve several functions at any given moment and can at times balance conflicting functions. Laver (1981) has indicated that polite openers generally have three key functions. First, they "defuse the potential hostility of silence in situations where speech is conventionally anticipated" (Laver 1981:301). Second, uncontroversial words serve to set up a comfortable context for further interaction. Third, polite openers allow the persons involved to move toward common ground as topics and roles are negotiated. "The greater degree of risk to face, the more constrained the options for mitigatory polite behavior become. . . . In other words, maximum risk leads to maximum routine, and conversely, maximum routine reflects maximum risk" (Laver 1981:290).

Relevant Studies

The rules of conversation seem to be a part of, and perhaps at the center of, language development from its very beginning. Hakuta (1976) indicates that a child learning a second language may use routines frequently because of a greater need to communicate. The child may use them as conversational crutches to help until greater language ability is achieved. A study by Hatch (1978) notes that adults use a discourse model as much as possible. That is, they learn to predict what will be said and to move a topic along by using questions. When the topic is fixed, they then have a listening grid to better focus on the conversational possibilities.

Perceived fluency is also pertinent to managing conversations. Sajavaara and Lehtonen (1978) found that native speakers spoke with more false starts, extraneous words, rephrasings, and imprecise, incomplete sentences *but* were perceived as being more fluent than nonnatives. Native speakers also used more fillers and other strategies to give themselves time to think. Nonnatives, on the other hand, simply used pauses or repetition, as these were the only two ways they had learned to cope with such situations. Another study by Sorhus, cited in Coulmas (1981), looked at spontaneous Canadian speech and found that a fixed expression occurred, on average, once every five words, or 20 percent of the time. The special emphasis of that study was on hesitation words, e.g., "you know" and so forth, that seemed to help speakers buy time in order to better articulate their thoughts as well as filling up the uncomfortable silence.

These studies reflect the realities of spoken communication and bring us to the heart of the matter: Conversational management strategies can aid second language learners in overcoming various hurdles they face in acquiring the language *and* can aid greatly in altering the perceptions of native speakers about the learners' fluency and general communication ability. The implications for the classroom are profound.

The Classroom

If the task of second language educators is to help people better communicate with one another through language, it would seem imperative to include instruction in cultural patterns of perception and thinking as well as increased emphasis on cultural styles of speaking. If that is true, then much more attention may have to be given to the flow of communication that takes place in the classroom. As Kramsch has pointed out, "although formed of grammatically correct sentences, most of the exchanges in language classes are highly unnatural in terms of discourse rules" (1981a:1). Traditionally, the communicative cards have all been stacked in the teacher's favor. The teacher controls the selection of speakers and topics, can interrupt at will, and is the conversational boss who decides who will speak about what, when, and in what way. Students are left with the rather reactive role of repeating what has already been said or in responding to patterns or requests for information.

The learners are sometimes put into no-win situations; once they have learned how to create new sentences, they are made to realize that they lack the conversational power to speak those sentences.

Learners need at least three abilities in order to achieve conversational power. They are the ability to view conversation as a partnership, the ability to use English as a way of getting things done, and the ability to take risks in communicative situations. A conversation without a partner is merely a monologue or a double monologue. Conversational management strategies can help to build the links that lead to a communicative working together. As Loveday has put it:

> The signalling of these roles (speaker/hearer) is essential because it provides the supporting framework for talk and carries meaning in so far as its absence can be taken as indicating lack of interest, coldness, etc. (1982:117).

The second point simply states that language learners need to be able to initiate and remain actively engaged in communicative situations that are meaningful to them. They need to use the tools of language to make things happen. For this to come about, of course, means that the teacher must give the students some opportunities to do more than merely respond to directions. The third point hints at a difficulty prevalent among ESL learners. As Kramsch has noted:

> Students of a foreign language are often intimidated by the competitiveness of the conversational context. Each speaker speaks without really responding or reacting to the other's statement; each takes care not to interrupt and not to repeat. In fact, neither one is able to listen attentively, for they are formulating their own future statements (1981b:95).

Our role as educators in this regard is to get the learners involved in a very active way in acquiring and using the conversational management strategies they are deficient in and in utilizing English as a lively tool for communicating.

Language learners need to know that conversation contains elements of both cooperation and competition. To be effective, one must be able to give one's partner proper cues and yet, at the same time, be ready to diplomatically take the floor and maintain a hold on it. Since most intensive English programs have students from a plethora of cultural backgrounds, considerable juggling may be required. Students from East Asia, for example, will probably need much work in making their speech patterns more direct and assertive, while those from the Middle East will probably need some help in toning down their argumentative styles, from decreasing the number of strategies used to softening those they do employ. There are many ways to work toward these goals. Those reluctant to get involved in discussions can be given responsibility for advocating or rejecting a certain position. Those inclined to argue and interrupt at every junction can be given responsibility for reducing conflict and finding ways for arguing parties to come together. Simulations of United

Nations gatherings or debates on controversial topics can help learners focus on communicating effectively, both verbally and nonverbally, in English. The use of conversational management cards, with each student having a card with six or seven different strategies, can be helpful in getting them to focus on how they say what they say. The use of such cards also helps learners to listen more attentively to the cues given from the other participants. (Each card would have one way of expressing each of the following: opinion, persuasive attempt, redirecting the conversation, tentative disagreement, sharp disagreement, concession, and/or any of a number of others. Each person would then be committed to using the specific strategies on his or her card and would be hearing slightly different phrases from the other people.)

Pursuing these kinds of changes in conversational styles puts the teacher, and the program, at the forefront of cross-cultural communication *and* conflict resolution. Conversational patterns share the same deep roots of cultural patterns of thinking. The goal is not to make everyone American, but to give our learners the conversational and conceptual tools with which to communicate more smoothly and effectively in the United States. For the ultimate benefit of our students, then, these strategies might be combined with discussions on cultural patterns. This would give the students opportunities to explore their ever-widening cultural horizons in a relatively non-threatening environment. It would also help them to enhance their observational skills in finding out what is happening around them. If we, as teachers and administrators, can help learners to go beyond their culture-bound ways of thinking and speaking (as we at the same time try to stretch our culture-bound patterns), and give the language skills needed to adapt to the new language and culture, we will have progressed a long way on the path of better cross-cultural communication.

BACKGROUND DISCUSSIONS

Cultural Conflicts in the Classroom: Major Issues and Strategies for Coping

Kristine L. Fitch
University of Washington

Teachers of ESL have unique experiences with and perspectives on cultural diversity. Cultural differences are part of the learning situation itself; students bring with them styles of learning and expectations of classrooms in general, which may be quite different than those of the teacher. Within any class there may also be vastly disparate styles and expectations. This variety is at once a challenge and, often, a frustration. It is frequently seen as one of the most significant rewards of the profession: Cultural differences may add to, and become an important part of, interaction between students and their teachers. On the other hand, when they do appear, cultural conflicts can rarely be ignored. They may pose a serious threat to a teacher's objectivity toward particular students. They may disrupt the learning process altogether when students of different cultures are unable to work together because of conflicts in values and behavioral norms.

A common exhortation of language teachers is that language does not exist in a vacuum; it may only be meaningfully studied in the context of a culture which uses it to communicate. Additionally, when English is taught as a second, rather than a foreign language, there are necessarily cultural differences between the teacher and his/her students. Surely it would be ethnocentric—and almost certainly ineffective—for a teacher to insist upon students' learning culture along with language and yet refuse to open herself to learning about theirs.

The author would like to acknowledge the assistance of Martha Clough, Maryann O'Brien, and Carol Archer in the development of this discussion.

51

This discussion will outline pressure points which may cause cultural conflicts, discuss strategies for dealing with conflicts, and propose a range of solutions, focusing on appropriate levels of teacher involvement in the process. All of this is with the hope and conviction that cultural differences and conflicts may become productive learning experiences in an ESL classroom. First, however, it may be helpful to posit more specifically the possible effects of such conflicts on classroom interaction.

Effects of Cultural Conflict

With the premise that cultural differences are part of ESL classroom environments, it is important to stress that they are potentially a very positive part. Students are often fascinated to have classmates from all over the world. Part of the reward of teaching culturally diverse groups is seeing students form strong friendships regardless of language barriers, exchanging insights from widely different perspectives, and, as a teacher, expanding one's own world view on the basis of those insights and perspectives. The ESL teacher constantly views herself in terms of contrast; there are continuing opportunities to understand one's own identity as an individual within a particular cultural context (Irving 1984).

Thus, positive effects of analyzing and exploring cultural differences in the context of an ESL class include creative tension and stimulation. Since cultural differences seem to cause breakdowns in communication as often as do linguistic ones, teachers are rarely at a loss for touching, sad, or funny anecodotes at gatherings when the usual opening presents itself: "OH, you teach FOREIGN students. That must be very (choose one): trying, interesting, difficult." It is all of those; it is never boring, and cultural differences are much of the fuel for the fascination.

When dealt with ineffectively or ignored, however, cultural conflicts can have drastic consequences. Learning may be disrupted by continual negotiation of personal battles, for example. Students may refuse to work together or withdraw from class interaction; and the tension created by such polarization may severely limit cohesion within the rest of the group. Teachers burn out when class after class becomes a battle of wills. Stereotypes may be maintained or strengthened by personal contact, rather than modified. New stereotypes and negative expectations for the future may become crippling self-fulfilling prophecies.

Through careful analysis of a problem situation, the teacher can direct efforts toward resolving it that, hopefully, will produce the positive, strengthening effects described first, rather than the destructive effects described later. It is important to begin this discussion of cultural conflicts, and the classroom disruptions they may create, with the assumption that negative repercussions of cultural differences will be rare occurrences.

Some Causes of Conflict

Two general themes emerge when discussing cultural conflicts with experienced teachers. One is the difficulty of separating such conflicts from those based on personal incompatibility; the other is reconciliation of different expectations of classroom behavior and interactions between teachers and students whose previous educational experiences have taken place in culturally different settings.

In the former area, when someone annoys or disturbs us, or does something which seems incomprehensible, a natural reaction is to observe that *that person* has done something strange or unacceptable. Further analysis of the situation may lead to the conclusion that the action in question was irritating due to a cultural difference rather than personal pique. Yet, scholars have never defined precisely what constitutes a culture and what is idiosyncrasy (Gudykunst and Kim 1984). Unsurprisingly, then, the line dividing the two is narrow indeed. If a Texan becomes irritated when a friend raised in Ohio addresses the Texan's parents by their first names, is the irritation due to violation of a Southern custom—a family norm—that no one addresses people of an older generation by their first names unless specifically invited to do so? When a teacher adores a sweet Chinese student who always does her homework and never argues, is he/she reacting to a cultural trait or discovering his/her own need not to have his/her authority questioned?

The effects of both personality and cultural conflicts are enhanced by the amount of contact between teachers and students, which in ESL contexts is often considerably more than it would be otherwise. It is difficult to like or dislike anyone very strongly if you are seeing them only a few hours a week; yet ESL students may spend five or six hours a day together, and an hour or two with each of their teachers, so that relatively minor interpersonal tensions may become greatly exaggerated.

In general, expectations for behavior may be seen as a template formed by previous experience. Individuals vary in the complexity and flexibility of their expectations. Their reactions when expectations are violated, and the degree to which they are consciously aware of them, are also extremely varied and affect the extent to which subsequent behavior is influenced by previous expectations (Brophy and Good 1974). An inescapable point of difference in ESL classrooms is the range of expectations, based in diverse cultural backgrounds and previous experiences in educational settings, which teachers and students bring to their interactions. It seems most fruitful to first examine students' expectations and their possible ramifications, then to explore the area of teachers' expectations and the concomitantly greater influence they may have on classroom interaction.

Students have definite expectations of their classmates' and teachers' behavior. Even those who have intellectually prepared themselves for dealing with a totally unfamiliar environment may be floored by the behavioral realities of the ESL experience. They may lack the perspective and tolerance for violation which comes from repeated exposure to different expectations. They may also feel powerless to change the situation, a constraint not often placed on the teacher. A student may be horrified by a peer's shouted disagreement with the point he is trying to make, for example, and wait helplessly for the teacher to control the outburst. If the teacher is accustomed to the volume and intensity of particular cultural groups' verbal behavior, he/she may never characterize the situation as out of control and, in fact, may be pleased at having created such a stimulating discussion. Alienation of the offended student and hostility toward the teacher for his/her apparent lack of authority may well result from such a situation.

An expectation which many international students apparently bring to the United States is one of freedom from the authoritarian educational systems in their countries; they believe that American democracy carries into the classroom. North American values of relative informality and seeming disregard for status differences may appear to confirm such assumptions. Yet numerous confrontations in ESL programs result from this belief. Students have on occasion voted not to use the assigned textbook, to have their lab instructor replaced, or not to attend an unpopular conversation class, and then calmly notified their teacher of their decision with the apparent expectation that this was all that was required to effect a change. While few teachers wish to be dictators, even North Americans must assume that they know more than their students in most areas of curriculum decisions.

Considerable evidence exists as to the influence teachers' expectations of individual students' behavior may have on the students' learning (see Brophy and Good 1974 for an extensive review). Unfortunately, such research tends to concentrate solely on children, perhaps with the assumption that adult learners' self-concepts are already well-formed, so that their performance is not greatly affected by teacher expectations. I would argue, however, that self-fulfilling prophecies can have impacts on interactions at any age level, and that second language learners' self-concepts are challenged in new ways by culture shock, and by language learning itself. The effects of teacher expectations on their adult students' performance are worth examination.

One type of expectation which may be especially influential in ESL classrooms is that of stereotypes. Many teachers, with perhaps considerable overseas experience and continuous contact with individuals very different from themselves, may feel immune to the blinding limitations of stereotypes. If defined only as unquestioned assumptions, this is probably true: faced with numerous situations during daily activity which violate previous expectations, teachers learn that any and all stereotypes are fallible. They may become accustomed to questioning assumptions and readjusting them in light of new information and experience. Yet, a stereotype may be formed in several ways: through previous experiences and contact or colleagues' information, as well as through lack of first-hand information (Garcia 1984). It is unlikely that human beings ever stop attempting to predict events based on their past experience; and expectations based on cultural membership amount to stereotypes. ESL teachers should assume that they will always have stereotypes present in their belief structure, try as they may to view each student as an individual. If continuously modified by ongoing experience, stereotypes will at least be complex clusters of cultural characteristics informed by a multitude of exceptions, rather than unidimensional, rigid expectations.

In terms of more general classroom norms, ESL teachers rapidly become aware of differences between the ESL classes they teach and the university classes in which they were students. Yet ,if punctuality, silence when someone else is talking, and only tactful, genteel disagreement of students were norms in those early classrooms, those will be expectations carried into the classes they teach, no matter how many times this fails to occur. Such expectations will be modified by experience; like stereotypes, however, it is unrealistic to assume that they ever completely disappear.

When analyzing classroom conflicts or tensions, it may be helpful to narrow down their causes in terms of the pressure points outlined above. Beyond the two very broad categories of cultural/personality differences and expectations for behavior, the following points may provide useful steps in analysis of conflict situations.

1. **Know Thyself.** The process of becoming aware of one's own stereotypes and expectations is similar to a fish attempting to minutely examine the chemical composition of its pond. Sources such as Stewart (1972), Freeman and Kurtz (1969), Kaplan (1970), Louv (1983), and Louis Harris and Associates (1975) offer insightful starting places for inquiry into American cultural characteristics. Descriptions abound of particular cultures' backgrounds and norms, as well as contrasts of those cultures with United States culture. Some are little more than travelogues; others offer extensive descriptions based on rigorous research. A few examples of the latter type are Wolff (1968), Das and Bardis (1978), Barzini (1971), and Condon and Saito (1974). Additionally, former students often prove excellent informants when encouraged to reflect on their experiences and interpretations from a more removed perspective, and relieved of the necessity of maintaining a peaceful relationship with their teacher.

Thus, teachers should seek to be as consciously aware as possible of their own stereotypes and expectations. Similarly, if a student has made a bad first impression during the first few days of class, it may be difficult to readjust that image in light of subsequent events. Definition or description of what actions caused the negative reaction and conscious contrast to later, improved behavior, can help to realign expectations. It is important to be specific about actions that trigger negative reactions. A few students, for example, have seemed to me to look bored during the first few days or weeks of a new term: they slouched in their chairs, looked out windows, sighed heavily and frequently, talked to their neighbors—in general seemed completely uncaptivated by my efforts to teach them. My instinct was to write them off as unmotivated or know-it-alls. When talking to some of them later on, many said they were overwhelmed by the newness of the city and the school. To hide the terror they felt, they devoted efforts to seeming nonchalant. I had assumed they would be scared; what put me off was the apparent ease of their adjustment.

If unsure whether a student's behavior is irritating because of a personality conflict or a cultural difference, check with colleagues. Do they have the same problem with that student? How do they react to it? Does the student's behavior seem to them typical of someone from that culture, or does it strike other teachers as unusual? Compare your reactions to that individual with others from the same culture. Is there somethng about Germans in general that you find aggravating? If there is, and you have contact with Germans term after term, it may be necessary to explore your own reactions more deeply, either with a colleague or a professional counselor, and plan constructive ways to deal with them. A helpful resource for beginning this self-exploration is Curwin and Fuhrman (1975).

As mentioned previously, a key consideration regarding stereotypes is to be clear about which ones influence one's own belief system. Once aware of stereotypes, it is helpful to remind oneself constantly of the exceptions: the assertive, talkative Chinese female; the flirtatious, lazy Japanese; the timid, hardworking Italian.

To minimize conflicts based on taken-for-granted expectations, teachers and program administrators must be careful to make their own expectations explicit as early as possible. The North American value placed upon indirect expressions of authority (Stewart 1972) is a frequent barrier to communication in this respect, both linguistically and culturally. When an ESL student is told "Why don't you move your chair over here closer to me so you won't be tempted to talk to Jose," the message to stop talking to Jose is rarely received. Orders should be worded as orders, not requests; not only is the grammatical structure more comprehensible, the statement is recognized as one requiring a specific response rather than truly offering a choice. This became clear to me when I urged a group working on a project to stop gossiping and get down to business with the observation that "if you don't quit visiting and get down to work, you won't get anything done before class is over." They smiled politely and nodded at me, the gossip continued, and sure enough, nothing got done that day. I was furious; the students were puzzled by my anger. They had understood the words completely; what had *not* been communicated was the speech act of demanding that they do something different from what they were doing. The students honestly felt I was offering a suggestion, which they were free to act upon or ignore as they saw fit. Make expectations clear at the beginning of the term or assignment, even if they seem obvious, such as "I expect you to get in your groups and work on this project. Do not spend time visiting." or "Take out a pen and paper and take notes on what I am about to say." Transgressions should be corrected gently, but directly. "Juan, put that away." "Get to work now, please. Do not talk about anything but this assignment."

2. **Be Aware of Students' Relationships.** It is often tempting, especially when teaching adults, to ignore tensions building between students, even

56

when they are obvious. Because they *are* adults, we may assume that they can, and should, resolve their own differences. Too often, however, they make no such assumption. In many cultures, outside arbitrators are such a part of argument that without them conflicts may never be resolved. Similarly, if the tension is due to home country hostility, the parties may be convinced that they were never meant to exist harmoniously in *any* context and that anything less than continuous aggression would be disloyal to their parents and country. In such cases, the wise teacher will ask questions and pay attention to all he or she hears and sees going on between students. Many times, only intervention from the teacher will defuse the situation enough to keep it from disrupting class.

A teacher told, for example, of an instance in which two male students were roommates—a softspoken Chinese and a flamboyant South American. They hated each other and were desperately trying to get reassigned to other dorm rooms, but in the meantime carried their feud into class: taunting each other, making veiled threats of after-school violence, refusing to work in the same group. As time went on the situation got worse; other members of the class began to take sides, and the barbs got increasingly vicious between the two principals. "I ignored it for too long," the teacher now reflects. "When I finally did talk to the Chinese about the situation, he told me he was so tense he hadn't been able to eat. I knew the Latin's work had really suffered, but I thought he was just partying a lot—I never made the connection with this conflict the two of them were having. You know, you figure it's none of your business, and taking them aside and telling them to keep it out of class doesn't usually work. Finally, I had one of them transferred to another class. Each of them could then make friends who didn't know each other, they could move in different circles, they didn't have so much contact, and things got better. At least my class could go on without that distraction."

Age differences and the role expectations incumbent upon them in different cultures may also cause friction, as with a student who interrupted *everyone*, including a middle-aged Indonesian woman who then considered it her duty to correct this bad habit. Students seeking romance or friendship, while endearing, may unwittingly step on cultural taboos surrounding relationships and be puzzled and hurt about why they are unpopular. Again, such interpersonal concerns should not carry over into the classroom; nonetheless, they often do. Teachers should be aware that relationships between students can enter the domain of their responsibility, and not let fears of being a "busybody" keep them silent until the situation has begun to interfere with learning. Similarly, when stereotypes among students become evident, they should be examined openly and countered with accurate information.

The exception, however, is that differences which surface in the first few days of the term are best left alone. If politics or personal antagonism come up that early in class, change the subject or squelch the discussion—let it resurface when students know each other better.

3. **Remember the First Priority: Language Learning.** In spite of the close relationships often formed in an ESL class setting, no self-respecting teacher should ever allow class to become an encounter group. Teachers are not meant to be therapists; any who fancy themselves as such are both deluding themselves and cheating the students of the learning they paid for. Teaching and learning language should always be of primary importance; cultural conflicts should be dealt with in the classroom only when they threaten to interfere with that process.

Yet the line at which an annoyance becomes interference is often a difficult one to draw. There are many students who will irritate a teacher, for example; but surely all do not hamper teaching effectiveness. Some signs of when irritation has become disruption are the following:

a. The teacher dreads class time, even though well-prepared, because it has become a struggle to maintain order.

b. The teacher restructures group exercises into individual ones because of relational tensions.

c. One or a group of students is ostracized by the rest.

d. Correction of behavior patterns becomes a daily part of class interaction, and the corrections involve the same behaviors every day (e.g., homework not done; constant chatter or giggles; barbed remarks or obvious slights; unexplained tension; constant, unexplained lateness).

Having discussed common pressure points of cultural differences and given the guidelines for analysis of conflicts (isolation/definition of problems), we are ready to take the next step of outlining solutions to cultural conflicts.

Solutions to Cultural Conflict

The problem-solving strategies described below are arranged along a continuum of teacher involvement, from little or no overt attention to the conflict by the teacher to active, introspective, carefully planned intervention.

1. **Defuse/Avoid the Problem.** This can frequently be the most constructive approach, especially, as mentioned above, in the early stages of a class's interaction. When a personality conflict, rather than a cultural difference, seems to be the underlying agenda, it should usually be dealt with in this manner.

Yet avoidance refers here only to classroom interaction. In many such instances, it is helpful to deal with the individual(s) involved outside the class. Begin with some kind of praise, and then describe your perceptions of the situation. For example: "Jose, you really are such a smart guy. I know you must have been a very good student in Peru. But sometimes, it seems like you try to answer every question that comes up. Sometimes I haven't finished the question before you've started on the answer." Have data to support your observations; describe specific, recent behaviors that illustrate the point. Then talk about the effect this has on you and/or the rest of the class. "I start to feel angry that I can't finish my sentences; and I'm concerned about the rest of the class; they never get a chance to show me what *they* know." Finish the discussion with a direct statement of the change you have in mind: "Let me finish my questions and let the other students answer sometimes, please."

If two students seem to be on touchy terms, follow the same steps. Talk to them privately; state your observations that lead you to believe they are having difficulties; express your feelings (concern for them, distraction or anger when it comes up in class). Encouraging both students to describe their perceptions of the issues involved may bring out productive discussion of their cultural expectations and their feelings about seeing those expectations violated. If it seems to be a personality conflict (these two people wouldn't like each other regardless of each one's cultural background) how deeply you encourage them to describe their versions of the conflict and their feelings about it will depend on your relationship with them and how comfortable you feel doing so. Usually, some spleen-venting is a good idea, but you shouldn't have to break up a fistfight. Be clear about the effects their quarrel has on you and the class, and about your expectations for their future behavior. As a last resort, separate them into different classes or call on an administrator to lay down the law.

2. **Confront/Express.** When cultural differences between the teacher and students or between groups of students have reached a point where tension is present in every class period, a simple ventilation of the feelings may do wonders to smooth the way for the rest of the term. Unfortunately, this can be a very threatening situation for a teacher and sometimes the students as well, and great care must be taken that such an interaction does not damage relationships beyond repair.

One very experienced teacher told of a class she had that seemed strangely frustrated by the textbook they were using. "I had used that book for that level before, and I really didn't see what the problem was. I tried different explanations; I gave them extra practice exercises. They always seemed to understand in class, but then almost no one did the homework. Or one person would do the homework and I'd see them all out in the hall frantically copying just before class. They started to seem real lazy to me, or dumb, maybe.

"Finally, one day when I tried to collect homework as usual, there wasn't any. I just stood in front of my desk and looked at them. You could feel the tension. I said something like 'Okay, what's the deal here,' and they exploded. They all started saying at once that this book was too hard, that they weren't able to do the work, that I never explained anything, never helped them at all, that they couldn't do it by themselves. They felt like they hadn't learned anything during the whole semester—and on and on. I sat there and nodded, my heart racing, of course, wondering what would I do now? Would I get a new book? Would I assign less homework? Would I become a cocktail waitress? Since I had no idea, I just nodded and agreed and paraphrased—'I can see that makes you very angry.' 'I'm sure it's very frustrating to feel you've wasted your time so far.'

"This went on for, oh, five minutes, which seemed like a lifetime, of course. Finally they talked themselves out. Then I told them I felt sad that they were so frustrated and angry, but that they were very smart, hardworking students and I thought they could learn a lot from this particular book. I didn't respond to the truth value of anything they had said about me; I just said, 'Well, let's back up a little and try again another way.' I put them in groups of two or three to do the homework assignment that had caused all the trouble, and sure enough, they could do it. I walked around and helped a lot, patting backs, touching every person that I felt it was safe to touch—all the females, the Latins. Things got a lot better after that. Instead of just explaining something and throwing homework at them, I started putting them in groups every day and encouraging them to work together. What I figured out was, I felt like they ought to be able to do it all by themselves, like it was cheating somehow if they worked together. They were used to being able to study with classmates; but here, they couldn't get together in the evenings. I learned a lot about group cultures and individualism that day."

A confrontation situation should always be controlled and brief. Screaming, violence, or personal attacks should not be tolerated, and venting of feelings should never become a regular facet of classroom interaction. Once in a semester may be enough; regularity will decrease the impact of such communication. The teacher should be prepared for anger and hostility, even directed at her or him, and must resolve to be calm and not take comments personally. As the teacher did in the situation described above, it helps to react to feelings, not to whether specific charges leveled are true or false. Finally, there will not be a solution to every problem. If Asians are insulted and put off by the dress and male-female interaction patterns of Latins, they will almost certainly continue to be so, even after an opportunity to voice their opinions. Yet the act of venting emotions, even negative ones, can increase each group's sensitivity to the other. It may even open the way to further exploration and sharing of perspectives. The teacher may or may not choose to become involved in that stage of resolution; if he does, cultural learning may become part of language acquisition.

3. **Increase Awareness Through Learning.** In this stage of teacher involvement, cultural differences are used as resources to teach. This requires a certain amount of class time and advance planning, as well as familiarity of the teacher with the cultural values and characteristics involved. While the students should be the informants, the teacher cannot be asking wide-eyed questions about a particular holiday or custom at this juncture. The idea is for the class to explore a culture's belief systems as bases for behavior; in short, to understand and appreciate as fully as possible why this custom or behavior makes sense to the members of that culture.

This is not meant to imply extensive effort toward development of a shiny new "culture unit" to work into the semester at some point. In fact, the more smoothly a cultural learning experience can be integrated into classroom activities, the more realistic it will be. Culture is a part of human beings, as well as language; if cultural learning starts out looking like a writing, reading, or grammar exercise, so much the better.

60

For example, a gifted conversation leader told of a class he had taught which included a Middle Easterner with unusually strong body odor. The man had become a class joke and was increasingly isolated from his classmates, who tried to avoid working in groups with him. They grew less cautious, as time went on, about hiding their snickers and remarks about his odor. The leader chose a class activity which involved selecting items from a list one would keep if marooned on Mars; and one of the possible choices was soap. The Middle Easterner left that off his list, to a louder-than-usual chorus of giggles. When the leader asked why, the man said that in his religion cleaning one's body or clothes with chemicals was a sin against God. He said that cleansing himself with only natural substances like water and sand made him feel closer to God, and that using soap would make him feel as guilty as would drinking alcohol. His classmates lapsed into shamefaced silence, recognizing his odor as a sign of a devoutly religous person, not just a filthy slob as some of them had thought. The leader thanked the man sincerely and went on. Nothing more was said, and though the man was not instantly loved by all his fellows, they stopped making fun of him and included him more often in their conversations.

In another instance, a teacher counted on a reading about marriage customs in different cultures to develop into discussion of nonverbal norms for males and females. He talked some about areas of behavior—how close one stands when talking to someone of the same or opposite sex, whether touching people of the opposite sex was acceptable and under what circumstances, eye contact, and so forth. Then he asked the students to give examples from their cultures. One semester, as two Thai women acted out a conversation to demonstrate how far apart they stood, one half-jokingly turned to a Latin man and said, "See? That's why I can't stand to talk to you. You stand on top of me and you always touch my arms. No man ever touched me before but my father." The Latins in the class were, of course, astonished and became much more circumspect in their touching behavior.

For culture learning to work so smoothly into class, however, the teachers in both cases had to plan ahead. They knew what points needed to be made, and they scheduled exercises or subjects which would make such topics seem like natural digressions. One teacher says she especially counts on vocabulary with -ist, -ism, -ity endings because they flow so easily into naming religions: Hinduism, Buddhist, Christianity, etc. "From religion you can go anywhere," she points out, "and I tailor that discussion to whatever differences are most pronounced, or are causing friction, in each class." It is crucial not to settle for simply a description of a custom; probing for the belief behind it can be a valuable source of insight for both cultural insiders and outsiders. It should be reiterated at this point, however, that teachers must be sufficiently familiar with the cultural characteristics and values likely to surface to ensure that the discussion will proceed in productive directions. Great caution must be exercised so that teachers do not open a Pandora's box of negative evaluation and perhaps ethnocentrism in the attempt merely to generate a stimulating discussion.

This paper has explored the general issue of conflicts occurring in ESL classrooms which are related to cultural differences existing both between teachers and their students and among the students themselves. Two pressure points were suggested that complicate the environment in such classes: personality conflicts, which are at times difficult to distinguish from cultural ones; and differences in expectations for various facets of classroom interaction. Three guidelines were offered for teachers to focus their analysis of cultural conflicts: be aware of their own biases, stereotypes, and expectations; be aware of students' relationships; and deal with cultural conflicts with the goal of making them part of language learning. A continuum of teacher involvement served as a basis for discussing the range of solutions available: from ignoring a conflict with the goal of defusing or avoiding it; to confronting the problem and encouraging the principals to express their perceptions and feelings about the matter; to actively incorporating cultural differences and even conflicts as part of language instruction.

While no discussion of issues or set of guidelines can cover every possibility of classroom interaction, it is hoped that this essay will provide at least some basic tools for analysis of cultural conflict. Perhaps the most crucial aspect of effectively dealing with cultural differences in ESL classes is constant attention to the "spice" they can add to students' and teachers' experiences. Someone once observed that life would be awfully boring if everything went right all the time; surely ESL teachers should feel safe from the possibility.

INSTITUTIONAL APPROACHES

Macalester College: The American Language and Culture Program

ELLEN D. COMER
Macalester College

The following essay describes the American Language and Culture Program at Macalester College, which was developed with a grant from the Exxon Educational Foundation. The Exxon grant has enabled Macalester to develop a unique ESL program that successfully prepares foreign students for their life and work at the college. According to students' evaluations, the extensive attention paid to all aspects of their adjustment process has resulted in a more successful overseas college experience than occurred when attention was paid only to language instruction. Moreover, the foreign students have not been the only people to benefit from this program. The entire college community has deepened its involvement in and understanding of the foreign student population at Macalester, thereby strengthening the college's international perspective.

Background Information

Macalester College, a four-year liberal arts college located in St. Paul, Minnesota, has long been known for its emphasis on internationalism. This emphasis is reflected in the large number of internationally oriented courses in the curriculum in general and, specifically, in the international studies major, the extensive study abroad program, and the presence of approximately 200 (12 percent) foreign students representing a wide variety of nations. Of these 200 students roughly half enter the college needing instruction in English as a Second Language. In order to meet this need, Macalester has developed a specialized curriculum in ESL designed not only to improve students' fluency in English, but also to provide a means for their successful integration into the cultural and curricular milieu of the liberal arts college.

The overall goal of the American Language and Culture Program, which was first instituted in 1981, is to combine ESL instruction with cultural/curricular orientation. This is accomplished by providing classroom instruction on the American character in addition to providing a variety of supplementary programs and activities designed to contribute to the students' understanding of life in the United States. The total American Language and Culture Program consists of the ESL Program, including two seminars focusing on life in the United States; a four-week field experience when students travel to a specific area of the United States; a team experience pairing three foreign students with one American student; special faculty advisers for each student; and a variety of supplementary activities. All of these components, with the exception of the ESL program, which has its own coordinator, are supervised by a program coordinator.

1. **ESL Program/Culture Seminars.** Macalester's ESL Program offers intensive language instruction on the intermediate and advanced levels. These levels correspond to the following scores on the Michigan Test of Aural Comprehension (AC) and the Michigan Test of English Language Proficiency (ELP):

Intermediate: AC = 45-65
ELP = 50-65
Advanced: AC = 65-90
ELP = 65-90

All ESL courses are credit-bearing courses. On the intermediate level students are required to take the following courses: Development of Reading Skills, Conversation and Comprehension, Intermediate Composition, and Cultures in Contrast Seminar. On the advanced level students take: Advanced Composition, Critical Reading, Seminar Techniques, and the American Language and Culture Seminar.

The overall goal of the two culture seminars is to provide, concurrently, active involvement in the exploration of cultural issues and meaningful practice in all language skills. Whereas the language practice in the other ESL courses concentrates on a particular skill area, the culture seminars provide multi-skill language practice. The content of the seminars is integrated into the other ESL courses, thus providing reinforcement and a unifying thread for the total program. The language-learning experience is approached as a whole process rather than as the acquisition of a series of different and sometimes seemingly unrelated skills.

2. **Cultures in Contrast Seminar.**

a. *Objectives.* Cultures in Contrast, the intermediate-level seminar, operates with two principal objectives in mind. The first of these is that each student should understand the most important cultural factors underlying American behavior in a variety of common social situations. Students examine the broad range of linguistic and social options Americans choose from to satisfy their everyday needs. They also examine the variables such as age, sex, education, social class, and cultural background which determine an individual's behav-

64

students simultaneously compare and contrast the various ways of behaving in their own cultures. Of primary concern in meeting this first objective is to help the foreign students understand why Americans act in certain ways but not to communicate a message that the American approach is in any way better than that of other cultures.

The second objective is to develop in the students the practical skills necessary to function appropriately, both socially and linguistically, in common social and academic situations. The social adjustments necessary for foreign students to succeed in the United States are often given only cursory attention during orientation sessions; after that, students are left more or less on their own. By paying specific attention to these problems and providing actual practice in appropriate verbal and nonverbal behavior for an entire semester, students' adjustments have proven to be far smoother, of shorter duration, and less painful.

b. *Description of Course.* The content of the Cultures in Contrast Seminar is organized around the following topics and focuses on the readings and exercises in two textbooks, *Beyond Language* by Levine and Adelman (1982), and *Communication and Culture* by Gregg (1981).

  (1) Culture, Reality, Stereotypes, and Expectations
      Gregg, Chapters 1 and 2
  (2) Verbal and Nonverbal Transmission of Culture
      Levine, Chapters 2 and 3
  (3) Personal Relationships, Gender Roles, Dating
      Levine, Chapter 4
  (4) Cultural Conflict and Cultural Adjustment
      Levine, Chapters 9 and 10
  (5) The Family
      Levine, Chapter 5
  (6) Education
      Levine, Chapter 6
  (7) Work Values
      Levine, Chapter 7
  (8) Intra-Cultural Variety, Food
      Gregg, Chapter 6
  (9) Time and Space
      Levine, Chapter 8
      Gregg, Chapters 3 and 4

c. *Suggestions.* It is extremely important for students to understand that the objective of this course is not to Americanize them but rather to facilitate their adjustment to the United States, thereby enabling them to have a richer, smoother overseas experience. The following quotation from James Michener (1975), which summarizes the basic philosophy of the course, provides a useful introductory exercise leading into the course objectives.

"If you reject the food, ignore the customs, fear the religion, and avoid the people, you might better stay home: you are like a pebble thrown into the water; you become wet on the surface, but you are never part of the water."

Also critical to the success of the course is the concept that no culture is better than another. The continued emphasis on a cross-cultural, non-judgmental examination of behavior is extremely important.

It is also useful to remind students frequently that this course is not just a content course but a language practice course. The activities designed to supplement the course content outside of class are useful in enabling students to use the skills taught in class. The following list of in-class activities suggests ways that the various language skills can be practiced:

(1) listening to lectures from guest speakers (video-taped for added reinforcement), taking notes, and summarizing lecture notes,

(2) taking objective and subjective exams,

(3) interviewing,

(4) giving individual oral presentations.

d. *Adaptations.* At the beginning of the semester, students are shown the following paradigm, outlining the four areas they will be exploring:

(1) What you think about Americans

(2) What Americans think about themselves

(3) What you think about yourself and your country

(4) What Americans think about your country

If it is not possible to devote an entire class to teaching culture, the use of this paradigm as a focus for the work done in other courses can aid in the students' adjustment and personal growth. For example, in a reading class selections could be chosen which would focus on areas 2 and 4 of the paradigm, whereas in conversation or composition coursework could address areas 1 and 3. The unifying thread provided by the content of the culture course has proved invaluable in developing a tighter ESL program. This same thread could conceivably be woven through other skill courses without having the separate culture course.

3. **American Language and Culture Seminar.**

a. *Objectives.* The advanced level culture seminar, entitled The American Language and Culture Seminar, is also designed to explore cultural issues while providing meaningful language practice. It forms a bridge course between the ESL program and other academic courses. The specific goals of this course are to acquaint students with the historical, social, and political values which comprise the "American character"; to enable students to explore how these tenets are reflected in various institutions here in the United States; and to enable students to synthesize knowledge of the American character from various primary and secondary sources in original essays, oral reports, and class discussions.

b. *Description of the Course.* The content of this seminar provides a more in-depth analysis of historical and cultural issues. The following topics provide the general focus for the course.

(1) American Diversity
(2) Immigration and Ethnicity
(3) Basic American Values
(4) Social and Political Change
(5) Government
(6) Education
(7) Sports
(8) The American Family
(9) American Business

The textbook, *The American Way* by Kearny, Kearny, and Crandall (1984), provides a useful focus for the course; however, it must be supplemented with additional readings in order to provide a more varied perspective on the issues being explored.

Of central importance to this course is the student research project that comprises a major portion of the final grade. Students are required to write a ten-page report of some aspect of American culture which they wish to explore in great depth. They are required to gather data both from library sources and from research conducted in the community, specifically from observation or interviews. The three main purposes of this project are to validate or debunk the cultural information taught in class; to develop the skills needed to locate, organize, and synthesize information from library sources, the mass media, personal observation, and interviews with people in the community; and to become better acquainted with the Minneapolis-St. Paul area.

This project enables students to become more familiar with American culture and to establish useful contacts with Americans in the community. It also provides practice in writing a paper similar to regular academic papers, and it provides an opportunity for the practice and improvement of all language skills.

Also important to the success of this bridge course is the inclusion of guest lectures, most of which are given by faculty members. The students benefit from exposure to differing lecture styles and also hear a variety of expert opinions on various issues.

c. *Suggestions.* Again, it is important to remind the students that this is a language course wherein the development of their English is equal to if not more important than the acquisition of cultural information. This course is not necessarily as cross-cultural in its orientation as the first seminar is; therefore, it is necessary to provide a balance of positive and negative facts and opinions in order to avoid a one-sided chauvinistic presentation of this culture.

d. *Adaptations.* In order to provide a multi-skill language practice course which could serve as a bridge course between ESL and academic courses for those students who resist studying more about American culture beyond the first semester, we devised a course with a different content focus but with similar goals. The title of this course was the Current Affairs Seminar.

4. **Interim Term Program.** Macalester operates on an academic calendar which includes a one-month Interim Term during January. During Interim students choose from a range of on- and off-campus courses and independent projects. As part of the Exxon American Language and Culture Program, students at Macalester may elect to travel on a 25-day bus trip to a selected region of the United States

a. *Objectives.* The objectives of this cross-cultural journey are to experience the diversity of United States cultural and economic life by visiting various institutions and landmarks typical of a specific geographical region, to continue developing language skills, and to develop an awareness and understanding of all the cultures represented in the traveling group.

b. *Description.* The trip, which is designed for approximately two-thirds international students and one-third United States students, provides an opportunity to visit historical and cultural sites, to experience American family life via homestays, and to share insights with fellow travelers from different cultures. The students participate in group activities during the day and are free in the evenings to become acquainted with families.

Students are required to keep daily journals in which they comment on their homestays, sites visited, and other experiences. They are also required to complete a final report designed to increase their knowledge of each other's countries and to promote general interaction among the group members. Students select a topic of interest (i.e. political structure, women's roles, etc.), and then interview other students on the trip about the topic. The information gathered is written up and submitted upon return. In addition to the project, first and second year students are assigned intercultural essays to read and summarize. Third year students read relevant passages about areas visited (from Garreau's *Nine Nations of North America* (1982)) and then respond to the readings.

The group stays with host families whenever possible and this aspect of the experience has proven to be a very important part of the trip. Families provide meals (breakfast and dinner) and transportation to and from the central meeting place in the mornings and afternoons. Attempts are made to locate families of varying socio-economic and cultural backgrounds. Some of the more interesting family experiences have included a stay with Amish/Mennonite families on farms in Pennsylvania-Dutch country, lower income black families (mostly single parent) in Memphis, Mexican-American families throughout Texas, and some Native American (Pueblo Indian) families in Santa Fe. In some cases, food stipends are arranged to help the families with expenses; however, most families are happy to volunteer. Families are not expected to entertain their students since the students' goal is to experience everyday life, but many times families do plan outings with their students and/ or social events with other families. Generally two students stay with each family. Information is sent to each city so families can choose the students whom they want to host.

Typically, the group meets in the mornings at a central meeting place and then buses to the activity for the day. Free time is worked into the schedules. The bus driver drops the group off at a meeting place in the afternoon, (usually 5 p.m. to accommodate working host families). In each city, the group is provided with an overview of some sort (general city tour, film, etc.) during the beginning of the stay so that students can explore specific areas of interest.

The trip is completely self-supporting; the student price includes transportation, accommodations, breakfast and dinner in most places, a textbook, and all group activities. Students pay their own incidental expenses. In the cities where the group does not stay with families, students receive a per diem food stipend. Some aid awards are given based on financial need.

A student assistant is chosen to accompany the leader. This student has received a larger aid award in exchange for his/her help in initiating activities to promote interaction in the bus while on the road.

c. *Suggestions.*

(1) Itinerary. As much information as possible should be gathered prior to determining the itinerary. Travel agents and Chambers of Commerce are useful resources.

(2) Transportation. Transportation arrangements must be made early in order to determine the cost per student. The cost for a 40-passenger bus with driver has varied from $7000 to $13,000. It is important to find a driver who will remain for the entire month, be flexible about the schedule, and deal well with the unexpected.

(3) Locating Host Families. International organizations are good starting places for names of possible families. Chambers of Commerce, AFS International Intercultural Programs, Rotary, NAFSA volunteers, the National Council for International Visitors, college alumni, and churches are also useful sources. Arrangements should be begun at least four to five months before the trip.

(4) A pre-departure orientation session is important for setting ground rules, going over the itinerary, and getting acquainted. A debriefing experience upon return allows students to evaluate their experiences.

(5) It is important to obtain liability waivers for the group leader and for the college and to make certain that students have adequate health insurance coverage.

d. *Adaptations.* This trip can be adapted for any region of the country. By having a faculty member sponsor the trip, it could have a specific focus based on the faculty member's field of interest (historical focus, sociological, etc.). A student worker could be hired to do much of the correspondence but should be supervised closely by a staff member.

5. **American Assistants.**

a. *Objectives.* The main purpose of this component of the program is to enhance the integration of the foreign students with American students. Each semester a small group of American students is chosen based on their interest in working with foreign students and their desire to expand their cross-cultural communication skills. Each American is assigned to work with a group of three or four foreign students from the Cultures in Contrast Seminar. The Americans' role in this group is to serve as tutors, peer counselors, and resource people. In the eyes of the foreign students, these American assistants can seem more accessible and non-threatening than the academic advisers or teachers. For that reason, the assistants are able to play a valuable role in the foreign students' adjustment process. The assistants are also an important agent in introducing the foreign students into the social milieu of the campus.

b. *Description.* As part of the credit the assistants receive for this practical experience, they are required to meet a minimum of once a week with their group. At these meetings the assistants conduct exercises designed to supplement the material covered in the seminar that week. They are required to keep a summary in lesson plan form of the activities for each week as well as a journal of their personal reactions to the formal meetings and to any informal or spontaneous interactions they have with the members of their group. To plan for their group meetings, each assistant must attend a weekly meeting with the other assistants, the supervising faculty member, and the Exxon Program Coordinator.

In addition, the assistants are required to write a mid-term and final evaluation of each of their students, commenting on the progress, level of participation, attitude, etc., of each. These evaluations serve to alert the seminar teachers and the program coordinator to any serious problems.

Lastly, the assistants are required to write a final paper on a topic of their choice. This project involves interviewing students in order to gain insights on a specific aspect of internationalism. Topics have included adjustment problems of a specific culture, customs of various cultures, attitudes of U.S. students to foreign students, evaluations of the program, etc. Emphasis for the projects is on the practical application of the information gathered.

c. *Suggestions.* Special instruction provided by the program coordinator and the faculty supervisor on how to structure a small group learning session is very important. Without knowledge of the necessity for some overall goals and structure in small group sessions, the American assistants tend to design only "rap" sessions which are generally less productive.

d. *Adaptations.* In lieu of having a program coordinator or faculty sponsor supervise the American assistants, a student intern can be used. This person should have experience in developing and implementing small group activities and in working in a cross-cultural environment. (See Appendix for a job description used to recruit student interns at Macalester.)

6. **Classroom Supplements.**

a. *Objectives.* A primary factor contributing to the success of this program is the large number of activities designed to supplement the classroom learning experience. These activities, which support and augment the coursework, serve to integrate language instruction, academic content, and practical experience. Through these activities, the students are provided an opportunity to practice their language skills outside the classroom. Conversely, they are able

70

to use the ESL courses as a place for interpretation of and feedback on the ideas gathered outside the classroom. All of these aspects of the program have been organized and implemented by the program coordinator.

b. *Description.*

(1) Speakers. At the advanced level, the seminar is supplemented with faculty and community speakers. This is an aspect of the program that has been extremely popular with both the students and the guest lecturers. Students respond well to exposure to a variety of teaching styles, and the lecturers have been enthusiastic about the chance to interact with international students. Many faculty members have developed a new appreciation for the amount of energy a nonnative speaker of English must expend in order to compete in an English-speaking classroom.

(2) Field Trips. In addition to the weekly activities with their American assistants, the ESL students are offered a variety of field trips. Whenever possible these trips are planned to coincide with the content of the seminar (i.e., a tour of the capital during the government unit, visits to various schools during the education unit). Students have enjoyed visits to various churches, museums, theaters, historic landmarks, businesses, and other areas of the city. The goal of these visits is to provide an opportunity for students to explore as many facets of the culture as possible. Some trips are required for class; others are made optional.

(3) Host Families. Upon arrival, students are able to request a host family. These families often include their students in family functions and serve as general resource people. Attempts are made to match student and family interests, and family professions with student majors.

c. *Suggestions.*

(1) Community Activities. It is useful to be on the mailing lists for local museums, theaters, etc., in order to be well-informed of community events. Many organizations will provide guest speakers at no charge. Local media will often provide video tapes of special programs which can be used in the classroom.

(2) Recruiting Host Families. Local churches, newspapers, schools and organizations can all be used as resources for possible host families. An information form completed for both families and students is a great aid in matching compatible pairs.

d. *Adaptations.* The coordination of all of these supplementary activities is a time-consuming task requiring special staffing. In the event that such staffing is impossible, one suggestion is to create a student internship (for credit) or work-study position to organize and supervise these activities.

7. **Faculty Advisers.** The advanced level ESL students enrolled in the American Language and Culture Seminar are each assigned to a faculty adviser in their intended major departments. The primary purpose for this special advising system is to familiarize each student with his or her major as it is practiced in the United States, as well as to provide an early link between

the ESL student and the academic department. The advisers provide accurate information about the general course of study for that particular major and about general academic policies, procedures, requirements, and options at Macalester. By providing this necessary information, the advising system contributes greatly to the successful integration of the foreign students into the American liberal arts education system.

a. *Description.* Throughout the semester, the advisers meet with their small groups of ESL students on a bimonthly basis for the purpose of orienting them to academic life in the United States. Students greatly appreciate the opportunity to become acquainted with an authority in their academic discipline. Since ESL students are sometimes very eager to begin their studies in their major, this contact has proven to be very satisfying for them while they must still take ESL courses. The advisers gain insights into the foreign student adjustment process and into the difficulties of overcoming language barriers.

b. *Suggestions.* This advising system has been most effective when instituted in conjunction with the advanced level seminar since the students' English proficiency is higher and they are more likely to have determined their majors. It is useful for the program coordinator to conduct periodic meetings with the advisers to brief them on effective advising techniques and to plan educationally and socially valuable student activities. Advisers are encouraged to invite their advisees to visit some of their courses. This often satisfies the ESL students' curiosity while exposing them to a variety of teaching styles and often reinforces the need for further English instruction.

c. *Adaptations.* Faculty members already serving as advisers might volunteer their time for periodic small group meetings with the ESL students. These advisers could perhaps speak to the seminar class as a whole.

The author wishes to acknowledge the following people for their contributions to the continuing success of the program: Lynne Ackerberg, Kim Brown, John Knapp, Pat Peterson, Tom Rowland, Karl Sandberg, David Sanford, Beth Willman-Van der Weerd.

Appendix
Internship Description

I. Title: Program Coordinator.

II. Department: International Center/Linguistics

III. Qualifications:
1. Upperclassman preferred.
2. Experience in developing and implementing a variety of group activities and programs preferred.
3. Cross-cultural awareness and sensitivity required.
4. Ability to work well with students, faculty, staff, and community resources required.
5. Demonstrated responsibility, initiative, and independence required.

IV. Duties:
1. Meet weekly with small group of student assistants and instructor for the "Cultures in Contrast" intermediate-level English as a Second Language (ESL) course. Provide leadership in planning out-of-class activities to supplement coursework.
2. Communicate regularly with instructor of "Cultures in Contrast."
3. Attend "Cultures in Contrast" at least twice a week.
4. Arrange and participate in out-of-class trips. (Arrange transportation, times, places, contacts, etc.)
5. Arrange occasional guest lectures for class. (Establish contacts, arrange videotaping, place, etc.)
6. Plan occasional social events for group of international students in "Cultures in Contrast" and for their American student assistants.
7. Participate in international student orientation and placement process of international students into English as a Second Language courses. This takes place the last week of August.
8. Assist in evaluating American student assistants' work for the "Cultures in Contrast" course.

(These assistants register for a tutorial through the Linguistics Department and receive credit for their work.)

INSTITUTIONAL APPROACHES

Ohio State University:
The American Language Program
Cross-Cultural Training Project

TIMOTHY TODD DIEMER
Ohio State University

Most teachers agree that language learners are not likely to do well if they are shocked, fazed, or stunned by the demands of cultural adjustment. The close relationship between skill in cultural adjustment and second-language development is obvious from the point of view of many language teachers. Experience in the classroom tends to show that when someone is adjusting well to a foreign culture the task of the teacher is easier and evidence of language growth is clear.

Staff at the Ohio State University's American Language Program have organized materials and conducted training activities that are intended to speed language acquisition by supporting cross-cultural awareness. The purpose is to enhance the learning of those students who lack previous international experience and face both the task of adapting to life in a foreign country and the task of reaching language proficiency requirements. These cross-cultural training activities have been carried out during four successive academic quarters. This paper describes the methods and activities of the current training design.

1. **Methods of Cross-Cultural Training.** We began to organize materials for cross-cultural training by studying methods. Hoopes (1979: 3-5) has drawn the range of cross-cultural training methods on a line from a university model on one end to a human relations/sensitivity training model on the other. Information transfer is most important on one end, while introspection and group interaction is emphasized on the opposite end. In the middle of those two approaches is an integrated cognitive/experiential model. Cross-cultural training within our intensive English program is an effort to implement a middle approach by drawing from both experiential and cognitive learning resources.

Gochenour (1977:33) provides a definition of the experiential part of cross-cultural training that can be used with this model:

> That avenue to awareness and knowledge derived from the perception of existential wholes, effecting a change in the one experiencing, expressible primarily in processes of the appositional, and secondary to the propositional mode of consciousness.

Gochenour suggests that there are two distinct but complementary types of mental processes involved in learning about a foreign culture (1977). One is promoted through information transfer and the other is promoted through experiential learning. Our use of the cognitive/experiential model is aimed at developing two types of learning through training activities that combine selected reference information about adjustment to American culture with insights and skills students have gained from their own experience.

Promotion of learning through experience is an essential feature of the cognitive/experiential model. Students in our intensive English program are adults or mature adolescents who are likely to bring with them a portfolio of successful life experiences. The fact that these students are preparing for academic study in America implies in some cases an outstanding position within their own community. To assume that members of a learning group of this type have gained skill and awareness from their experience is consistent with a general principle of adult education (see Srinivasan 1977: 58), as well as a specific feature of the experiential/cognitive model of cross-cultural training. One advantage to our program of the cognitive/experiential model is the potential to train students to adapt their skills and perceptive abilities for use in new environments.

As Hoopes (1979: 3-5) pointed out, however, strict reliance on trainees' experience to develop cross-cultural awareness and skills may produce unsatisfactory results. Experiential methodology can limit the amount of content that can be presented. Sometimes it really is not possible to guarantee that plans to present certain content can be fulfilled. There is an expectation that a number of key concepts will be produced by the trainees themselves. The cognitive aspect of Hoopes' integrated cognitive/experiential model is meant to minimize limitations that might occur with a strictly experiential design.

2. **Content of Cross-Cultural Training.** Another advantage to our program of the cognitive/experiential model is the potential to balance content that the trainers consider important with that derived from asking participants to rely on their own insights and experience. As we planned a curriculum to reach this balance, we selected three content areas to include in the training design: a definition of culture, models of cross-cultural adjustment, and a condensed description of cultural values that influence American behavior. Our goal was to intersperse these three content presentations among related experiential activities.

The first content area, presentation of a definition of culture, was important in establishing how the term would be used throughout the course of training activities. Definitions of culture that have been used in the past within language programs range from "small c culture . . . the way people live . . ." to "large C culture . . . the major products and contributions of a society . . ." (Chastain 1976: 388). Further ambiguity may have resulted if our students translated the word into another language without an equivalent meaning. Since attendance at the sessions was voluntary, we attempted to announce each session in a way that would be clear and attractive. As we invited participation in the activities, we avoided even using the word "culture" until we could define how the term would be used within the context of the training. We found that a greater number of students readily understood the value of a session if it were announced as "English through drama" than if the same session were announced as "cross-cultural role play." Likewise, we found that a topic presented as "family relationships in your country/family relationships in the United States" produced more discussion than the same topic presented as "family relationships: cross-cultural comparison." When there was an opportunity to attach a specific meaning to the word culture, we asked the students to consider the following definition: "Culture is a way a group of people go about meeting life's basic needs."

To define life's basic needs, we turned to the work of Abraham Maslow (1954) and charted the needs in the following way: self-fulfillment, self-esteem, sense of love and belonging, safety, and physiological needs.

Although a definition of culture along these lines has its limitations (Condon and Yousef 1975), it became a useful standard during discussions of cross-cultural topics.

In addition to the presentation of a definition of culture, a second content area included as part of the training design was the presentation of two models of cross-cultural adjustment. The first model, which we called "Hills and Valleys," was developed from the idea that life in an unfamiliar cultural setting is characterized by more emotional highs and lows than life in a familiar cultural setting. Similar models using up and down or high and low metaphors have often been constructed for cross-cultural training, according to reports of former Peace Corps volunteers and AFS International Intercultural Programs returnees. In the model of this idea that we developed, an early peak called "happy daze" is followed by a deep valley called "me against them." The ups and downs of the model then get progressively less steep but never level out to the emotional equilibrium that can be found in the home culture. The second model of cultural adjustment that we presented, called "Seven Steps in Cross-cultural Adjustment," is based on a summary of the model built by Gochenour and Janeway (1977) which describes a path of progressive accomplishment in adjusting to a new culture. We decided to present the two models in order to describe cross-cultural adjustment as a process of continuous learning about and growth within a culture different from one's own. We wanted to show students that by studying the experience of others in similar situations it would be possible to recognize patterns or cycles or steps that could be expected as part of life in an unfamiliar cultural setting. This would provide our students with a standard to compare the individual experience of cross-cultural adjustment with what others had gone through.

An opportunity to present a third area of content arose when, as a reaction to training activities, participants suggested comparisons between America and another culture. With the topic set by discussion, we presented the third content area, a summary of descriptions of American culture by Stewart (1972) and also Condon and Yousef (1975). This presentation consisted of a short lecture and handout. In addition, students were encouraged to study about their own culture by interviewing compatriots or through research in the university library.

3. **Skills of Cross-Cultural Adjustment.** In addition to a goal to include three areas of content, we set objectives to build three cultural-adjustment skills. The three skills were identified as observation, willingness to take risks, and willingness to suspend judgment.

Our first objective was to develop observation skills. Although most of our students come to America with broad experience in learning through observation, the new cultural setting probably makes it difficult to know what to observe. According to the Gochenour and Janeway model of adjustment to a new culture (1977:17), the early stages lack "depth of perception"; it takes some time and effort for newcomers to reach a stage from which they can "observe what is going on and sort out meaning." At least a few of those who experience this early stage have stories to laugh about later, having had to wait for someone else to go in before being sure of the correct restroom door, for example. It is common for newly-arrived students to face cross-cultural challenges that no one has told them how to handle; in many of these situations observation is the most useful skill. One objective of our program was to develop this skill through training activities.

Another objective was to develop skill in choosing worthwhile risks and a willingness to take them. As for a child learning to walk or a teenager learning to drive, it is difficult for anyone living in a foreign culture to avoid taking risks. However, within a familiar cultural setting many of life's risks are predictable and it is possible to prepare for the consequences. Risks become complicated for those who have chosen to live and study in an unfamiliar cultural setting. Life's risks in the new setting may or may not be greater, but they are likely to be different and partially unknown. Whether a student is lost among strangers or confronted with love at first sight, new skill is needed to know which risks are worth taking. This was a second skill that we expected to develop through training activities.

A third objective was to develop a willingness to suspend judgment. The hills and valleys model of cross-cultural adjustment that we had presented charts an early period of "happy daze" in a new cultural setting followed by an opposite period of equally strong negative feelings. The students who experience this negative stage may perceive cross-cultural encounters as "me against them" and make frequent critical judgments. At a later stage a willingness to suspend judgment overcomes this negative period. Stewart (1972:79) describes the turning point:

> The individual is not likely to suspend judgment and action until he fully understands the strange ways (of life in a foreign country), since his own assumptions, values and habits are seen as normal, while he is likely to regard those of another culture as strange, undesirable, unnatural or immoral.

We included the objective of developing willingness to suspend judgment in an effort to bring students past this turning point.

4. **Implementation.** To implement the cognitive/experiential model with the content and skills chosen, we first considered the physical setting. We wanted students to think of these sessions as something different from regular classroom sessions. To do this, we looked for rooms with daylight instead of fluorescent tubes and upholstered furniture or seating on the floor instead of common classroom desks. When possible, we added food or drink. Several of the activities encouraged students to take different roles than normally occur in the traditional classroom, and we wanted the setting to suggest this.

Eleven sessions were scheduled during the course of an academic quarter. Here is a list of the topics used:

a. Needs assessment; nonverbal communication: cross-cultural gestures
b. Values that influence American behavior (short lecture with handout)
c. Role play: student/professor relationships
d. Definition of culture
e. Models of cross-cultural adjustment
f. Role play: balancing leisure time with study time
g. Folk wisdom: cross-cultural discussion
h. Attitudes toward time: discussion
i. Family relationships: discussion
j. Panel discussion with former students: insights on academic success in an American university
k. Simulation game: Mountain People/Valley People

Dates were announced a few days in advance, and invitations were sent out. Since participation was voluntary, attendance varied from only five students at one session to more than twenty at another. The schedule was set up to weave in and out of busy periods of other academic activities: formal language study, undergraduate or graduate school admissions procedures, and preparation for language proficiency tests.

This list of eleven topics is a revision that was prepared after we considered the results of the needs assessment conducted during the first session. We had asked the students to write down any expectations for the training and anything in particular that they hoped to learn. In fact, it was necessary to make substantial changes when we discovered that the most likely reason for a student to participate voluntarily in cross-cultural training was an expectation of practicing English. We changed most of the activities to make language practice a prominent feature.

Experiential training includes not only creating and enhancing new experiences but also making use of the learners' past experiences. Therefore, we began many activities with a technique to find out what the students already knew about the topic. For example, we assumed that the students came to the training with some knowledge of nonverbal communication and familiarity with a range of gestures. Rather than give students a description of American gestures for ordinary nonverbal tasks, we asked them to try out their own style within the group to see whether communication was effective (see exercise 1 in Appendix). In this way, some truly bicultural gestures were discovered. Some trainees had already learned a few typically American gestures, and so the accomplishment got recognition. Those who were used to quite different gestures learned from the experience how a cross-cultural misunderstanding could occur through a mix-up in nonverbal communication.

In addition to making use of what students already knew about the topic, the activities encouraged them to adapt their skills and experience for use in the new culture. For example, when dealing with government or university officials in familiar settings, most students said that they were confident that they knew how to be polite and tactful and still combine that with enough force and directness to get what they wanted. Through role play of student/professor exchanges and other likely situations, students practiced using those skills in an American context (see exercise 2 in Appendix). Discussion followed to gain opinions from the group about whether the same combinations of tact and force that were familiar in their own culture were appropriate in the new context.

The activities also provided practice with the specific skills of cultural adjustment written into the objectives. The simulation game, Mountain People/Valley People (adapted with new content from Experiment in International Living's East/West Game (The Emperor's Pot) cited in Hoopes and Ventura 1979), was intended to develop observation skill and demonstrate its importance in cross-cultural interaction. To set up the simulation, one group of students was given a task and a set of behavior rules (see exercise 3 in Appendix). A second group was given a different set of rules and an opposite task. To complete its task, each group had to find out through interaction and observation the rules that the other group was using. One student's comment after the game summed up the point: "When we go into a new culture, we have to pay attention."

We made it a point to notice in simulation games and also in what was said about everyday experience whether students were practicing observation and other skills of cross-cultural adjustment that were stated as objectives. One skill we noticed was a willingness to suspend judgment which developed during discussion of cross-cultural issues. Students accepted our guidelines for comparing cultures and discussed issues of similarities and differences rather than positive and negative aspects. One student described his own decision to suspend judgment this way: "There are things I don't like and don't agree with, but when I came here I knew things would be different and I have to accept that."

Participation in role play and simulation developed another skill of cross-cultural adjustment, willingness to take risks. Participation in itself represented a risk to most of our students because they were new to America and the American academic setting, and they were unsure of their English. We encouraged participation in the activities as an initial step, with the expectation that practice with cross-cultural role play and simulation would make it easier in the future to identify and take worthwhile risks.

One thing that became apparent about the cross-cultural training activities that we used was that they were effective in getting students to discuss the experience of life and study in America. A range of topics came up as points of cross-cultural comparison. An example of a concrete discussion topic was habits of eating; a more abstract topic was the existence and methods of the training itself as an expression of American culture. During the discussions, it was sometimes possible to illustrate concepts from the content areas we had presented. For example, when questions came up about why Americans do things a certain way, we referred again to the definition of culture and asked students to think of the behavior as a method for meeting one of the basic needs.

5. **Evaluation of the Training.** At the end of the training, participants were given a questionnaire asking what they learned, in what ways it was useful, and which activities ought to be repeated for other students. Experiential activities such as Mountain People/Valley People and the role plays rated highest. Students told us that the activities were thought of as something different within a week of intensive language study, and that was rated a positive feature. Many students reported that the activities were effective in providing practice in both the language and the cross-cultural skills needed in certain situations.

Other ways to evaluate the training are still being planned. At a later date, language teachers can be asked whether participants seem to have adjusted better to life and study in America than those who declined opportunity for cross-cultural training. For a more formal measure, improvement in scores on standardized language tests could be examined against a control group to determine whether there is a correlation between participation in this cross-cultural training and progress in language learning.

6. **Development.** Immediate plans for program development focus on locating and adapting additional training activities that will introduce content and provide practice with the skills that we have identified. Our process of finding and adapting training activities can be compared to international cooking: although Thai curry is made in Bangkok with bamboo and coconut milk, Thai-style curry can be made in Ohio with potatoes and cow's milk. The process is the same, but the content is changed a bit to fit the local situation. The ideas and materials presented here were useful at a certain time with one

of our student groups. Additions and revisions continue. Cross-cultural training within other intensive English programs can be set up by identifying appropriate training materials and adapting them to fit the needs of each particular learning group.

Appendix
Exercise 1.
Nonverbal Communication

Directions: Your assignment is to communicate the messages below without using any words. Choose a few of the messages below. Think of ways to communicate using gestures, or any nonverbal form. You will then be asked to communicate the message to the larger group.

Situation	Message
(You see someone you know on the other side of a busy street. You have some important news for him/her.)	"Come here, quickly!"
(You are watching TV with a friend.)	"This is really boring!"
(A stranger has asked you for direction to Highbanks Park.)	"I have no idea where it is."
(A teacher is waiting for you to answer.)	"Just a moment, please. I'm still thinking."
(You are skiing in the mountains.)	"It's really cold today, isn't it?"
(While driving your car, you have caused an accident. The driver of the other car is approaching you. He is very angry.)	"Calm down. Don't get upset."
(You are telling a friend some private information.)	"This is a secret. Be quiet about this."
(A teacher has given you an extra book to help you learn a foreign language.)	"Thanks very much. I am grateful."

Exercise 2.
Role Play
First Role—Graduate Student

You are a graduate student majoring in _____. You are a good student. You get good grades and usually finish your work on time. Recently, however, there have been some problems. Your car is broken and you must get it fixed. Friends from _____ are visiting for a week, and you must spend time with them. You have a part-time job and are working extra hours this week. The workload in your other classes has been unusually heavy. There is one assignment you will not be able to finish on time. You want to complete this project, but it will be about one week late. If you have an extra week, you will be able to do all the necessary research, and your project will be a good one. It will be impossible to finish the project by the deadline, which is tomorrow. You have decided to talk to the professor, explain your situation, and ask for a one-week extension of the deadline.

Second Role—Professor

You are an associate professor in the College of _____. First of all, however, you are an educator. You believe in the benefits of the old established system of education. There is a body of knowledge that is important to the profession. Your students must prove that they can master this body of knowledge. Part of their education is learning to be punctual and precise in their work. Sometimes students come to you and ask for special favors. Sometimes they ask you to extend deadlines or make exceptions to established policy. You seldom allow any exceptions or favors. If you allow one exception, it seems everyone asks for something. Deadlines, standards, and policies are an important part of education. You expect students to meet deadlines and follow policies. This will be required when they get a professional job. Once in a great while, you will extend a deadline or allow some other favor. But you will do this only for a good student who persuades you that this is necessary. In any case, you will certainly emphasize the importance of professional standards.

Exercise 3.
Mountain People/Valley People

Valley Society Instructions

Background: Your group is an advanced society from the valley. The mountain people have a valuable art treasure that is needed by your national museum. This piece of art is important to the mountain people, so they will probably want to keep it. However, the mountain people are poor and your society is rich. Your superiors in the government have instructed you to get the art treasure from the mountain people, and they will accept no excuses for failure. Your government has allowed a large budget, so you can offer the mountain people as much money as they want. Down in the valley where you live, little is known of the mountain people. You will have to learn how to deal with them, so that you can persuade them to give you the art treasure. Although the mountain people are poor, they are clever at trading, so you will have to be careful. However, you can assume that if enough money is offered, anything can be bought.

Procedure: The behavior rules of your valley society are described below. All your actions should follow those rules. Plan how to persuade the mountain people to give up the art treasure. Part of your group should climb the mountain and visit the people there. The other part should stay in the valley and receive the foreigners who are coming down from the mountain to visit you.

Description of valley behavior: 1) Greet by placing your hands on your shoulders and looking briefly towards the sky. 2) Stand far from those you are talking to, but face them directly, and look directly into their eyes. Hold your head high. 3) When you want to explain something, you can touch members of the opposite sex lightly on the arm or shoulder. Contact between members of the same sex is rude and must be avoided. Show anger or displeasure by clapping your hands loudly. 4) Be businesslike and serious. It is rude to laugh or make jokes during business meetings. It is also rude to eat or drink during a serious meeting. Be careful not to waste time. You can remind people of the time by frequently pointing to your watch. 5) Do not accept any decisions that are made by only one person. Others may have a different opinion. Everyone's opinion is equal. Find out what everyone thinks. Men and women are equal. Both must be asked for their opinions. 6) Hold up some money, a coin or a bill, as a symbol of your sincerity. You can emphasize the importance of anything by giving it a high price.

Mountain Society Instructions

Background: Your group is an ancient society from the mountain. Your people have a priceless art treasure that has been handed down from generation to generation. Protection of the art treasure is essential to the happiness and security of the people. You have learned that the people in the valley want to take the treasure from the mountain. There is no risk of war, but the treasure must stay on the mountain. Your people have always avoided war by establishing friendships with foreigners. Therefore, you must now establish friendship with the valley people so that they will give up the idea of taking the art treasure away. Up on the mountain where you live, little is known of the people in the valley. The elders say that the valley people are rich in material things but poor in knowledge of the more important things in life. For this reason, they may be confused about the meaning of friendship.

Procedure: The oldest male in your group is the leader. He will appoint a group to go to the valley and establish friendship. Others will stay on the mountain and receive a group of visitors from the valley. Behavior rules for your mountain society are described below. All your actions should follow these rules.

Description of mountain behavior: 1) Greet by shaking hands. Men should greet all other men; women should greet all the other women. 2) When talking to foreigners, avoid looking directly into their eyes. Stand close to them, but look down or to the side. Direct eye contact is rude. 3) Show friendship and good will immediately after greetings. Men can do this by smiling and placing a hand on another's shoulder. Women can also touch other women in this way, but men and women should never touch each other in public. Be friendly and lighthearted. Show happiness by laughing, smiling, and clapping your hands. 4) Before any business is discussed, make sure everyone is comfortable. Everyone should be invited to take a comfortable seat on the floor, and food or drink should be offered. Humor is the key to good relationships. Laugh and make jokes, and encourage everyone to join in. Business can wait. Friendship comes first. 5) Avoid any arguments with the valley people. Of course, you must not give them the treasure, but you should try to agree with everything they say. Do not give any direct yes or no answers. What they ask might be possible, perhaps some years in the future. For the present, friendship is most important. In any case, final decisions can be made only by the oldest male in the group. 6) Do not discuss financial matters. It is rude on the mountain to discuss money or politics. In fact, everyone uses checks or credit cards because the sight of money is offensive. Popular conversation topics are history, art, and philosophy.

INSTITUTIONAL APPROACHES

University of Wisconsin-Milwaukee: Cross-Cultural Component in an Intensive ESL Program

LAWRENCE BELL, PETER LEE, DIANE NELSON, AND RITA RUTKOWSKI
University of Wisconsin-Milwaukee

The new English as a Second Language student encounters many adjustment difficulties which may retard his/her development in learning a language and possibly jeopardize the success of his/her college career. While most colleges and universities offer orientation programs to aid the students in adjusting to their academic courses, very little is done to help them with the difficult initial problems of coping with the language, adapting to the new culture, and relating to people of various backgrounds and cultures. In the Intensive English Program at the University of Wisconsin-Milwaukee, this problem has been addressed through the implementation of a special cultural orientation component. This paper will describe the goals and organization of this component and outline its development over the past two years. An evaluation of the cultural orientation component will be given, and both foreign and American student reactions will be presented.

The University of Wisconsin-Milwaukee Intensive English Program is a pre-enrollment program administered through the College of Letters and Science. The enrollment varies each term, but the program averages from 80 to 90 students a semester. The language and cultural composition of the students in the program is approximately 30 percent Arabic speakers, 30 percent Spanish speakers, and the remainder a mixture of speakers of 15 different languages. Approximately 60 percent are learning English for academic purposes as opposed to 40 percent for career advancement. Some of the latter intend to return to their native countries while others will remain in the local community.

The program is divided into four skill areas (grammar, writing, reading, and oral skills) and classes meet four hours daily. Five eight-week sessions are offered a year (two each semester and one in the summer). Based on initial placement testing, students are assigned to appropriate ability levels within the program. The cultural orientation component that we will address here has been incorporated into the curriculum of the Intensive English Program. One oral skills class each week (with the exception of the first and last week of each session) is devoted to a cultural-orientation session.

The purpose of the cultural-orientation program is threefold: (1) for the international students, to develop a better understanding of American culture and values; (2) for the American participants, to develop a better understanding of the varied cultures of the international students; (3) for all participants, to stimulate a non-judgmental appreciation of all cultures and cultural differences.

The cultural orientation program consists primarily of weekly sessions on various topics chosen to stimulate discussion of cultural differences. Although these group sessions take place during the regular oral skills class hour, instead of the regular teacher being present in the room, it has been arranged for American students to join the class that day as discussion facilitators and participants. The facilitators are seniors or graduate students who are earning independent study credit through either the linguistics or communications department for their work with the program. The participants are students from the communications department's Intercultural Communications class. These students are involved in the project as an extra-credit option for their class. Their participation in these sessions as participants and the paper that they write about their impressions fulfill the requirements for their extra-credit project. This inter-departmental cooperative aspect of the program is one of the principal reasons for its success. The involvement of these student peers as cultural informants instead of teachers allows the discussion session to take place in a more informal, less threatening atmosphere.

The overall running of the program is taken care of by a committee made up of members of the IEP staff who have volunteered to work on this project as a part of their normal teaching/administrative load. This committee meets weekly to handle the organizational needs of the program (selecting facilitators, dividing students into the discussion groups, scheduling, etc.) and to prepare/revise the discussion materials.

What follows is a description of how the program has evolved and been adapted to better suit students' needs. We will also address the issue of evaluation and how we are trying to judge the success of the program.

The orientation program lasts 12 weeks and is based on a series of small-group discussions concerning intercultural issues. The discussions take place during the regularly scheduled oral skills hour of the Intensive English Program. The groups are kept small in size: a typical composition would be one facilitator, three American participants, and seven international students.

As mentioned earlier, the American students involved may participate in one of two ways: as a discussion group facilitator or as a participant of the group. The group facilitator's role is to guide the group from an objective point of view, ensuring that everyone has an equal opportunity to contribute, to raise appropriate questions, and to point out cultural differences, and in general, to keep the discussion moving in a productive manner without interjecting his or her personal opinion. As participants in the discussion group, American students play an equal and similar role to that of their foreign counterparts. They are, in a sense, contributing to the discussion as cultural informants expounding that point of view as a representative of the respective culture.

The reason it was decided to employ other Americans as facilitators and group discussion participants, rather than use the teaching staff of the Intensive English Program, was to allow the students to feel at ease and speak openly and honestly on sensitive issues. We felt that this change was necessary to enable students to relate on an equal basis with their American counterparts. This atmosphere, for a variety of reasons (out of politeness, respect, or fear), does not always exist between students and teachers in the classroom. So, in fact, during the cultural orientation discussion hour of the week, the regularly scheduled teacher is not present, and the discussion group facilitator solely directs the class.

During each of the 12 weeks, there is a different topic for discussion. Some of the topics were decided upon on the basis of demonstrated student needs and others were ones that the project committee felt needed to be included. Recurring themes and questions such as "Americans are cold and superficial," "Why do families kick their children out of the house when they're 18 years old?" "People from that country never bathe," and "Chinese people don't love their children," prompted us to include topics on the ideas of friendship, the family, and stereotyping and prejudice. Along with the discussion of the family, we provide the opportunity to spend a weekend with an American family for those students who want to participate in a home stay. This home stay component allows our students to get a glimpse of American family life and also provides them with a contact within the community. Other topics that our committee felt needed to be included in the discussions were experiential learning (the idea of experiential vs. academic learning, identifying learning resources, setting goals and doing regular self-evalution), culture shock (the stages a person goes through upon entering and discovering a new culture), language, and nonverbal communication. Discussion strategies and guiding questions are provided for the facilitators for each topic. However, we try to keep the guidelines broad enough so that both Americans and foreign students can approach the topic from a variety of angles.

The topics are generally ordered in terms of how much personal investment is required on the part of the group members. Those topics which involve less risk and investment are given early in the semester, and a conscious effort is made to establish understanding and a sense of security in the group. Specific activities designed to develop group cohesiveness are organized in each group to build this type of group dynamic. Later in the semester, when there is a feeling of mutual acceptance, topics which involve personal and cultural values and beliefs can more easily be discussed.

As an end to this general description section, there are two aspects of the program that should be mentioned, although they no longer exist. We feel that the experience that led us to review our program will be instructive for others trying to set up similar programs. The two major changes have to do with recruiting and training of facilitators and the dropping of an initial set of discussion topics on basic survival skills in a new culture.

When the program was first devised there was a perceived need for work with the newly-arrived students on such basic things as banking, the city bus system, and finding housing. We therefore set up a Phase I during which the group discussions would be devoted to these topics. It was thought that students who were not new would be able to help with providing information for those who were. In the first running of the program, several weeks were allotted for this Phase I. In the second and third runnings, in response to reactions from both the foreign students and the American students, Phase I was progressively shortened. By the end of the third time through, it was obvious that our original conception of Phase I was simply wrong.

It is not that newly arrived students do not have specific, powerful problems dealing with a strange banking system or renting an apartment. However, it became clear that trying to help with the solutions to these kinds of problems in a group discussion could not work. The problems that students had of this nature usually needed more than discussion to solve. Many times the students had family or friends to help them, someone from their own culture who had the experience to understand and mediate. Much of the time the new students were shy and reluctant or embarrassed to discuss these problems in a group setting. Often, the more experienced students were not happy devoting time listening to and discussing things they felt they did not need. For all of these reasons, Phase I was drastically reduced by the time we began the program the fourth time. Basically, it has become individually oriented, ad-hoc counseling whereby a student with a particular problem can be helped by one of the staff or by an experienced facilitator.

As for the second major revision, the sources for recruiting facilitators, as well as the training they receive, have undergone some serious changes since the initial program. In the early days, we felt that we could get by with people who were basically interested and willing to take on the responsibility of working with a group. At that time both facilitators and participants were recruited from the same undergraduate intercultural communications class offered in the department of communications. The students were given extra credit points for their participation in our cultural orientation program.

As we gained more experience with our program, we increasingly realized the crucial nature of the facilitator's role. We also realized that it was not realistic to expect undergraduates, often in their first encounter with people from other cultures, to be capable of handling this role as effectively as it should be. We are now recruiting as facilitators only graduate students with intercultural experience and/or experience in small group leadership. We have also instituted a required day-long training session for facilitators to familiarize

90

them with the particular needs of a program like ours. As has been mentioned, the facilitators now receive course credit (Independent Study) for the work they do with us. The American student participants (non-facilitators) in the groups continue to be recruited from the undergraduate class in intercultural communications.

During the first several sessions that the cultural orientation component was a part of the Intensive English Program, there were no formal evaluation sessions conducted. However, regular evaluation devices were incorporated into the sessions beginning with the fall 1983 semester. They were a part of the program both in the middle and at the end of the semester and took place in three ways: (1) a discussion session to help the groups focus on evaluation of group as well as individual goals; (2) a written self-evaluation by participants (both foreign and American) and facilitators of their experiences during the sessions, including any personal development that they recognized; (3) a written evaluation by the facilitators of the program sessions and topics in order to help determine their value and appropriateness.

In addition to these written instruments, we have incorporated more regular meetings into the Cultural Orientation component. We now have meetings every two weeks for the facilitators and the project organizing committee in order to distribute discussion group information and maintain a flow of feedback with regard to the successes and failures of the groups.

There have also been a variety of comments offered by students, facilitators, program developers, and instructors from both the Intensive English Program and the Communications Department. Many of these have already been discussed since these were the instigating factors for the changes that have been made from program to program. Such factors as the elimination of survival needs and the changing of topics, through both addition and modification, are examples of the way in which the evaluation has had a direct effect on the cultural orientation.

There are still changes that need to be made in the cultural orientation program, and the committee is continually evaluating both the negative and positive statements received regarding the program. The most formidable negative factor early on was the very high demand on staff time compared to the number of hours the students were actually involved in the program. This problem has been solved in part simply by running the program over several semesters and becoming more efficient in its planning and implementation. Another factor has also contributed to the elimination of this particular problem. The use of trained graduate student facilitators has greatly reduced the amount of time spent by the staff in troubleshooting and clarifying.

On the positive side, as a result of the evaluation process, we discovered that the program has been successful in initiating the beginning of non-judgmental understanding not only of American culture and values, but also of the variety of other cultures represented by our English as a Second Language students. We have presented both foreign and American students the opportunity within a non-threatening environment to discuss openly their conceptions of and questions about each other's cultures and values, as well as an opportunity to look actively at and explain their own cultural values.

Evidence of the success of the program comes through verbal and written evaluation from both American and foreign students. Participants have repeatedly expressed an interest in continuing with their same groups, feeling that they have developed a rapport with these fellow students during their group sessions. Foreign students completing the cultural awareness discussion groups in one session of the Intensive English Program have requested that new topics be added to the program in the next session so that they can again participate. Students, particularly the American students, have expressed an awareness of their own growth in self-confidence and a new feeling of comfort and ease in cross-cultural situations.

The positive feedback that has been received from the students involved seems to point to the success and value of the program. The following quotations from program participants illustrate reactions to the program by American as well as foreign students:

> One of the things I discovered about getting along with people from different cultures is that although all of us live in the same world but we have many different customs between each other. We can learn many things that we have never imagined. (Silvia Burrel, Mexico)

> In a sense, I came to the English as a Second Language discussion in hopes that I could contribute something to the discussion (perhaps something of a self-centered nature), but instead, I found myself listening and learning about cultures and perspectives that I could learn only by intercultural contact—or direct intercultural experience. I cannot say that I learned any one specific piece of knowledge or information, but perhaps I unlearned more than I learned. I feel that intercultural contact is a probable remedy for humanity's social disease: "hardening of the categories." I only wish that I had more time and opportunity to administer this remedy. (Susanne Lise Huth, United States)

INSTITUTIONAL APPROACHES

Intercultural Communication as an Integral Part of an ESL Program: The University of Southern California Experience

MICHAEL MAGGIO
University of Southern California

CHARLES W. GAY
Temple University-Japan

During the late 1960s and early 1970s, interest in application of Carl Rogers' (1951, 1961) non-directive client-centered counseling to the advisement of foreign students led to the development of the Intercultural Communications Workshops (ICW) by the National Association for Foreign Student Affairs (NAFSA). The purpose of these workshops was "to increase mutual awareness among the participants of the role their cultural backgrounds play in influencing their values, their behavior, and their perceptions of the world around them" (Althen 1970). Intercultural Communications Workshops were conducted on a number of individual campuses and also in joint workshops which included students, faculty, and staff from several campuses.

At about the same time, English language programs were seeking to provide natural communicative settings in which their students could speak English and improve their proficiency in the language while they were discussing matters of interest to them and to their fellow students. Even before the current research and theories of affectivity, faculty of English language programs realized the importance of affective factors in their classrooms. They knew that more natural conversation would develop if the students were allowed to discuss topics that directly concerned them.

At the University of Southern California (USC), a semester-long ICW was developed as part of the curriculum of the intensive English program. This part of the curriculum was called the "intercultural conversation" (IC) class.

93

The class was two hours per week and thus only a small part of the 25 hours in the intensive program, but those two hours turned out to be a very popular part of the program for students. They looked forward to the informality and to the chance to speak with American students. The class has been an integral part of the program ever since.

The class is designed to create a comfortable, relaxed atmosphere. To this end, it meets in a lounge rather than in a traditional classroom, and coffee and cookies are served to promote a feeling of sharing.

American students form an integral part of the program. Their presence allows the international students to meet their American peers with whom they will eventually need to interact on a daily basis. The American partici- pants are not peer teachers. However, they serve as both linguistic and cultural models, providing the international students with valuable information that can only be learned through direct experience.

A typical IC class begins with a warm-up exericse which actively involves the participants mentally and physically. Lining up in alphabetical order, for example, requires the participants to review the English alphabet and to interact with the other participants. Warm-up exercises are usually related to the topic of the session and help set the tone.

The warm-up exercise is followed by an experiential exercise which focuses on the topic of that session. The participants may be asked to gather infor- mation from the represented cultures, or they may be placed in situations which force them to experience the dynamics of a cultural problem. Occa- sionally, some participants act as observers, taking notes on the process of the interaction and later reporting to the whole group.

The experiential exercise is followed by a debriefing in which feelings are checked out and observations regarding the interaction are made. Through this debriefing the participants make discoveries about themselves, the other participants, and the cultural dynamics they have just experienced. This debriefing is followed by a general discussion on the implications of what has been observed, and then by other, practical exercises which give the partic- ipants a chance to apply what they have learned.

This format has been found to produce a maximum learning experience because it focuses on both the cognitive and affective domains. Originally, the IC class was more information oriented. The students were given handouts with vocabulary lists, questions for discussion, and other information that was felt to be pertinent at the time. However, it was found that these handouts detracted from the experience, focusing the students' attention on linguistic concerns rather than on cultural ones. As a result, the issues were dealt with on a cognitive level while the affective level was minimized.

Culture shock, like any other emotional problem, needs to be dealt with on an emotional level. Intellectualizing ignores the gut level reactions and leaves the victim of culture shock with no emotional outlet or resolution. For this reason, experiential exercises are used in the IC class whenever possible. These exercises allow the affective domain to be tapped and explored and,

94

when combined with more cognitive activities such as discussions, bring the participants to a greater awareness of their experience.

Experiential exercises are arranged progressively in terms of the level of self-disclosure. As trust and group rapport develop, the exercises become more demanding, and the participants are allowed to experience the unknown and often threatening dynamics of other cultures, but in a safe, controlled environment. Participants are never forced to reveal more than they want to.

Over the years in which IC classes have been offered at USC, a wide array of topics has been dealt with. In recent years, those topics have been narrowed down to what are considered the most essential. Here is an outline of the IC class currently offered each semester:

1. **Introduction.** Students become acquainted with each other. They are given a chance to show how much they know about the countries represented in the IC class.

2. **Hobbies.** Students continue to learn about one another. They share their interests and learn what they have in common.

3. **Crime.** While the focus is on crime in the United States, students share cultural perceptions on crime and punishment. Students then develop lists of ways to live safely and securely during their stay in the United States.

4. **Foreign Student Problems.** Problem-solving activities are used which deal with specific problems that foreign students have. Students are asked to rank solutions. Students then generate their own lists of problems that foreign students encounter. These problems are discussed and possible solutions are proposed. This session allows students to see that they are not alone in having adjustment problems. It is also very enlightening to the Americans.

5. **Verbal Communication.** This session deals with the problems inherent in verbal communication. The Rumor Clinic (Pheiffer and Jones, Vol. II) is used to get the session moving. While the major problem for foreign students is understanding and speaking in a foreign language, students come to realize that even native speakers have trouble communicating. Ways for more effective verbal communication are discussed and practiced.

6. **Nonverbal Communication.** This session focuses on proxemics, eye contact, and gestures. Differences are experienced and then compared and contrasted.

7. **Perceptions.** This session begins with personal perceptions and leads into cultural perceptions. Paul B. Pederson's Map Exercise (Weeks, Pederson and Brislin 1982) is used to introduce the concept of ethnocentrism.

8. **Stereotypes.** Through Allen/Maggio's Breaking Cultural Stereotypes Exercise (Pfeiffer and Jones, Vol. IX), students experience what it is like to be stereotyped by others. They also see how others feel about being stereotyped. Students are then given a chance to break stereotypes and to correct misconceptions that others have about their culture.

9. **Learning and Change.** The Learning and Change Exercise (Weeks, Pederson and Brislin 1982) is used to assess the effect of change on perfor-

mance. This leads into a discussion of culture shock, and students are given a chance to share their own experiences.

10. **Marriage and Family.** Differences in marriage customs are shared. Roles of men and women in different cultures are discussed.

11. **Impressions.** Present perceptions of group members about each other are compared to their first impressions at the beginning of the semester. Cultural as well as personal bases for these impressions are explored.

12. **Description.** Lyra Srinivasan's Cross-Cultural Study Prints are used to explore physical manifestations of a culture (Srinivasan 1977). Students are asked to bring objects from their countries, and the meaning and uses of these objects are discussed.

13. **Values.** The Parable (Hoopes and Ventura 1979) is used to discuss value differences. Critical incidents (Hoopes and Ventura 1979) are then used to introduce differences in values across cultures.

14. **Emotions.** Emotions are discussed on a general level. Students then share their own feelings, particularly those dealing with their experiences living in the United States and dealing with people from other cultures.

15. **Closure.** The group's progress over the semester is discussed and its termination is dealt with.

Student reaction to IC class has generally been very positive. They like the casual atmosphere, enjoy the various topics, and are happy to meet American students. Here are two typical reactions that students have had to the IC class:

Class is very free and comfortable. I like free talking so I like this class.

I like this class because it is a friendly class. I made many friends here. And it taught us many things which are very important, but we always miss them in our daily living. In this class I learned a lot about foreign cultures which I have never heard of before. Though it is a class it seems a conversation at home to me. I feel comfortable and relaxed in this class. I like the American teachers and American students in the class. I think I started to like America from this class.

As can be seen, the IC class has had many positive effects on the students. Since the class deals with cultural dynamics, it helps the students, most of whom have just arrived in the United States, deal with the effects of culture shock. The students begin to understand the dynamics of what is happening to them, realize that they are sharing common problems, and begin to deal with anger and confusion. Their feelings of loneliness and isolation are thus minimized. Instead of placing blame on some outside entity such as the ESL program or unfriendly Americans, they begin taking responsibility for their own feelings.

The American Language Institute employs two foreign student advisers (FSAs) who are also trained ESL instructors. The IC class is normally facilitated by those FSAs rather than a regular faculty member because the FSAs are trained to deal with cultural adjustment, can easily detect a student who is having problems, and can help him/her in the class and privately in the office before things get out of control. Because of his/her function as an FSA facilitating rather than teaching the class, his/her role as helper is readily perceived by the students. This tends to give the students a positive attitude towards the program. Facilitating the IC class has become an important part of the FSA's role at the American Language Institute because it gives a type of student contact which is essential to his/her role as adviser. Without that contact, student problems would remain unknown.

However, the IC class need not necessarily be facilitated by an FSA, and regular faculty members have been trained to lead it. The semester-long training is based on the trainees' attending the IC class as particpants so that they can experience the class on the same level as the students. This experience is then debriefed each week in an additional one-hour session which includes the trainees and the FSA only. In this session, the material used in that particular week's IC class is discussed in detail as well as student reaction and trainee reaction to it. Relationships among students and between students and trainees are also talked about with particular emphasis on such concepts as who leads a group and why and who dominates a group and why. In this way, trainees discover their individual group behavior and how it affects group interaction. Thus, democratic and authoritarian leadership styles are looked at in depth. In the writers' opinion, democratic leadership is essential for the success of an IC class, for it allows students to learn at their own pace, make discoveries as they are ready to, and take responsibility for themselves. However, it is also important for the facilitator to recognize his/her own leadership style and to be comfortable with it.

The American student participants, on the other hand, are not trained. It is very important that they be the peers of the international students, and any training would upset the balance of the relationship. However, these participants are carefully chosen. A notice is posted in the work-study office briefly describing the position and the qualifications. In order to be qualified, candidates must be work-study recipients (for budgeting purposes only) and should be native speakers of English. This native-speaker stipulation serves two purposes: a linguistic one, providing our students with native-speaker input; and a cultural one, providing them with a model of American culture. Occasionally, international work-study students are employed. However, their English should be exemplary and their experience with American culture such that our students can learn something from them.

Each candidate for the position is interviewed by the facilitators. The interview is used to determine the amount of interest the candidate has in working with international students. While no experience with international students is required, it is important that the candidate be sincere in his/her commitment to attending the IC class on a regular basis and that he/she be truly interested in learning about other cultures and in meeting people with very different backgrounds and points of view.

Those candidates who meet the facilitators' standards in the interview process are hired. They are briefed as to who the students are and what their purpose at USC is. They are also given a brief description of what to expect in the class. Otherwise, they are given no training and are thus allowed to experience the class on an equal footing with the international students.

In a class of about 15 students, an attempt is made to present a balanced picture of American culture. To this end, the facilitators try to employ men and women, minorities and non-minorities.

While it is difficult to find American participants, the success rate with those who have been employed has been very high. The American students generally learn as much from the IC class as the foreign students and often request to attend a second semester. However, experience has shown that using the same student for more than two semesters results in burnout.

As was mentioned above, the IC class is a two-hour block in a 25-hour intensive level English class known as ALI 200. Thus, only students who place into level 200 or who come up from the lowest level ever get to participate in an IC class. Students who take IC class, then, have either just arrived in the United States or have been here for one semester. Because of time constraints, students who place into the intermediate and advanced levels never get to take an IC class, although cultural adjustment is sometimes discussed at those levels. While it is recognized that these students also have adjustment problems, it is felt that they have enough proficiency in English to be able to deal more effectively with cultural adjustment, and those with severe adjustment problems are referred to an FSA. In addition, students in these levels are taking classes in their academic department so that they are being exposed to Americans and American culture. The intensive level students, on the other hand, are isolated from American students because of their lack of proficiency in the language and because all their time is spent in English classes. The IC, then, is much more important for these students and, with the presence of their American peers, serves as a bridge to regular university life.

TEACHER SOLUTIONS AND APPLICATIONS

Culture Partners in Symbiotic Education: U.S. and Foreign Students Learning Together

VERNIE DAVIS
Guilford College

Symbiosis refers to the relationship between two dissimilar organisms in close association, especially when the relationship is advantageous to both. Such a relationship is possible among foreign and American students when an educational institution views the presence of foreign students as an asset to the college community while being concerned about the langauge and academic needs of both. This paper suggests that by developing such a relationship between institutions (or departments within the institution) it is possible to create a learning environment for both groups. Since the paper is written by a professor of anthropology rather than by a representative of the language center or international education office, it may be particularly helpful in presenting the perspectives of those with whom ESL leaders and professionals in international education may want to join to enhance the benefits of symbiotic relationships.

This paper describes a project which pairs U.S. students in an introductory anthropology course with international students studying intensive English. The "culture partners" are provided with a structure within which to learn from each other to discover cultural meanings using the anthropological research approach of the ethnographic interview. The anthropology students are instructed in the principles and methods of ethnographic interviewing in their anthropology class and are assigned this project as one of their course

---

Although the project is described by the Associate Professor of Sociology/Anthropology at Guilford College, it was developed jointly with Ahad Shahbaz, Director of the Inter-Link Language Center, (an intensive ESL and orientation program at the College).

assignments (see Appendix for project handout). They are required to set up interviews with their assigned culture partner for one hour per week for nine weeks. They keep detailed notes of their interviews and use these notes to write an ethnography on some aspect of their partner's culture. The English language students are required to participate in this project their first semester and may elect to repeat it their second semester if there are enough students in the cultural anthropology class. There is a high rate of students choosing to repeat the experience. The Inter-Link Language Center director spends one class period on orientation and collects names and phone numbers of interested students. The anthropology course spends three class periods on the project and has one class reading related to the project. The anthropology professor assigns students their partners and deals with any problems locating partners at the outset. Thus, the program involves minimal administrative effort on the part of the English language center—a fact which, in retrospect, seems to indicate great foresight on the part of the Inter-Link director.

There are several reciprocal benefits to the project, each of which nicely demonstrates the validity of the West African proverb "the left hand washes the right." Not only do the two sets of students have the opportunity to learn about the culture of the other, but the interactive process of the project allows them to make important discoveries about their own cultures as well. The international students have a language partner with whom to practice English while they discuss culture, and the anthropology students are able to learn about ethnographic research and the importance of gaining the insider's perspective. Finally, as pointed out earlier, such joint projects reduce administrative and instructional time for instructors and administrators in both institutions.

A key element of the project has been the focus provided by the anthroplogy class. The course stresses the importance of ethnograhpic research which seeks to learn about a culture and describe it from the point of view of the participants of the culture. "Rather than *study* people, ethnography means *learning from people*" (Spradley 1979:3). One of the goals of this project is to help students learn what this kind of research is like. Prior to presentation of the assignment, students have looked at culture as knowledge and have explored how culture influences our perceptions and understandings. They thus understand that a central goal of ethnography is not only to avoid imposing one's own cultural interpretations and understandings, but to seek to discover those meanings that are important to the culture one seeks to understand. They are instructed to begin their interviews with what Spradley has termed a conscious attitude of ignorance. "I don't know how the people of Cushing, Wisconsin, understand their world. That remains to be discovered" (Spradley 1979: 4).

The students are instructed to use Spradley's approach to interviewing to elicit what Spradley calls Grand Tours and Mini Tours. To get the details considered important by the cultural guide, the anthropology students must let the cultural informant point out the important highlights of his or her own culture. In this case, students focus on life histories, explaining what it

100

was like to grow up in their culture. The students are instructed to keep detailed notes to which they can refer when asking for more information about items mentioned in the grand tour. These follow-up questions lead to the mini tours. In this method, it is important that the categories of discussion and the questions asked come from topics initiated by the informant so as to avoid asking questions based on one's own categories of meaning. In this way, the interviewers are assured of discovering concepts meaningful to the culture they want to learn about rather than framing issues in the context of their own culture. Students inevitably question this process at the outset since they cannot imagine ahead of time where it might lead them, but they gain an appreciation for the approach as they engage in the project. As one student put it:

> My ethnographic interview was not at all what I had expected. I anticipated a small man with dark complexion, eager for the chance to make an American friend. Enter a person six feet tall, two hundred and fifty pounds, light skinned and not the least bit interested in me or my country. What happened to the Lebanese guy I had signed for? I just could not believe the stereotype I had so carefully built could be that misconstrued. . . . The important questions I had intended to ask turned out to be so trivial that I was too embarrassed to even mention most of them.

Since accurate records are important in ethnographic research, the anthropology students are required to submit their notes for comments and evaluation after approximately three interviews. Throughout the nine-week period, a few minutes of an occasional class period are spent asking students about their interviews and helping with problems. Discussion of problems helps the students better learn the method of ethnographic research and provides an opportunity for them to learn from each other. One student, concerned that her culture partner from the Gaza Strip kept talking about all of the wars instead of his life history, came to discover through class discusssion that this history *was* his life. Not only did this particular Palestinian and the American Jewish student learn a great deal through each other, but class discussion allowed these discoveries to be shared with others in the class.

Toward the end of the nine weeks, a class period is spent explaining how to analyze interview notes to discover cultural themes. Spradley (1979) has several helpful chapters devoted to this issue. Students are asked to bring a list of themes to the next class. Discussion of these themes in class further shares cultural discoveries with the rest of the class, helps remind students that they must be careful about generalizing from their one cultural informant, and helps prepare them for presenting a written ethnographic description that focuses on a cultural theme.

The benefits of this project are several. In fact, students engaged in the project perceive additional benefits beyond those envisioned by the project designers, and students in the anthropology course have been highly enthusiastic about this project in the end-of-the-semester course evaluations. Recently, a student carried out an independent study to evaluate this project. Using the strategy of "illuminative evaluation" as developed by Parlett and Hamilton (1972), she conducted ethnographic interviews with both sets of participants to discover benefits they perceived.

The U.S. students benefited by (1) learning about a particular culture, (2) becoming aware of new cultural perspectives, (3) helping a foreign student practice English, (4) learning an important research strategy in anthropology, and (5) learning to take responsibility for their own learning. Frequently, the U.S. students were completely unaware of the existence of the country of their culture partner. Many students admitted that they had no idea where the country was on a map before the interviews (Harrison 1984). Besides the factual knowledge about a particular culture, students were able to learn firsthand one of the themes of the cultural anthropology course—the significance of culture on perception. Discovering these perspectives for themselves was a valuable experience for the students. One student observed in her ethnographic report that the project affected her understanding of her own culture. "Not only did I learn about her culture, but it made me think about my own. . . ." Another said, "It was a little bit difficult for me because I had to interview a Palestinian and I'm Jewish. So for me, I had to re-evaluate things of my past. But it has opened up my mind. I've never heard the other side before" (Harrison 1984:6). Harrison also learned that several of the U.S. students took pride in their role assisting someone learn English (though this was never an explicit part of the assignment) and that they took personal satsifaction in the improvement in English communication they observed with their partners.

One of the stated objectives of the project is to help the U.S. students learn about anthropological research by direct participation. This project helps those who may never take another anthropology course learn more about the perspective of the discipline and serves to interest others who had not previously planned to major in this field. Whether or not they do further work in anthropology, it serves to help students discover that all learning does not come from books and helps them take a more proactive relationship to their learning.

Benefits to the international students are (1) being able to talk about their own culture to an American who is a willing listener, (2) learning about American culture, (3) having an opportunity to practice English, (4) developing autonomy in interacting with a stranger without their English-language teacher, and (5) being able to make a new friend. Many of the students expressed their pleasure at being able to talk about their country to a North American. They felt that North Americans have little knowledge about their countries and welcomed the opportunity to clear up stereotypes. As one student put it: "Of course we are living with Americans, but we don't have a long time to talk about our culture. We want Americans to know about the things we have. . . . It is important to make our country known here" (Harrison 1984:4). Another said, "I accepted the interview because I like to talk about my country, my customs—everything about my country—as much as possible. I am really proud to be from my country, especially when I am so far from it" (Harrison 1984:4).

Although the interview focuses primarily on the cultures of the international students, the interactive nature of the method leads to many discoveries about U.S. culture. The international students make many observations based on the interaction with their American culture partners, e.g., differences in the meaning of friendship and the cultural freedom to talk about everything—politics, religion, customs, people, education, family, etc. Because they are discussing culture, it is easier for these topics to be discussed with the North American students. Frequently the friendships lead to contact outside of the interviews and include such activities as shared meals and trips to share some aspect of U.S. culture.

Because the interviews are in English and because the international students do a substantial part of the talking, there is considerable practice in communication in English. Topics of discussion are usually different from those in English classes and thus stimulate the learning of new vocabulary. The interviews provide a semi-structured setting which facilitates what for many of the international students is their first substantial communication in English with someone other than their English teachers. They approach the project with nervousness and trepidation and gain confidence in interacting with a North American.

Finally, many friends are made. As noted earlier, the international students are sometimes disappointed to learn that the American concept of friendship can terminate quickly and that the relationship is, in some cases, limited to the assignment and ends when the obligation ends. Nonetheless, friendships have frequently developed that have led beyond the assigned nine-week project, and both the U.S. and foreign students have found it easier to meet and interact with others on campus as a result of the project. They learned it was acceptable to be ignorant and that it was exciting and fun to ask questions and learn.

A note of caution may be advisable. Because both sets of students in a project such as this are human beings with their own cultural biases, interpersonal styles, and individual interests, there is a greater potential for personal problems than with more usual assignments such as library research projects. Both sets of students should be prepared to be culturally sensitive so as to be able to identify and correct cultural misconceptions. For example, the meaning of body language differs from culture to culture, and students may send nonverbal messages that are misinterpreted. Boredom, anger, sexual interest are prime areas for misunderstanding. Although many continuing friendships have developed from this assignment, international students should be warned not to be disappointed if the "friendship" does not continue after the assigned project. By alerting students to potential hazards, maintaining close contact for feedback from both sets of students, and encouraging students to turn misunderstandings into cultural learning situations by discussing them openly, project supervisors are able to prevent serious problems. It is also recommended that students be versed in ethical principles of ethnographic research regarding their responsibilities to each other (see Spradley 1979: 34-39).

One of the most striking aspects of the project is the fact that everyone benefits in a significant way. Not only do both sets of students benefit, but both sets of administrators have part of the work done for them by the other. No one is left feeling that he/she is doing all of the work or all of the giving while someone else collects the benefits. There are other ways to establish this type of relationship. The Inter-Link Language Center at Guilford initiated projects with residents at a nearby retirement home to create grandparent/ grandchild relationships between retired senior citizens and international students and with American students studying foreign languages as language partners. Again, there are symbiotic benefits for all parties. With sufficient imagination, there is probably no end to the possible projects that could be set up, each involving very little administrative effort on the part of the language center. Such symbiotic relationships in cultural education might even serve in the long run to provide models for more symbiotic relationships in cross-cultural politics and economics.

Appendix
Ethnographic Research Project
Student Instructions

The Interview

Life histories are a form of ethnographic research. Like all ethnographic research, the goal is to learn about a culture and describe it from the point of view of the *participants* of the culture. "Rather than *studying people*, ethnography means *learning from people*" (Spradley, 1979:3). Life histories are one of several approaches used by anthropologists to collect and present ethnographic data. Life histories are particularly useful in helping us learn about the life cycle—what it is like to be born in and live each phase of one's life in a particular culture. However, since cultural institutions touch the lives of individuals, I think you will be amazed at how much you can learn about cultural institutions—such as families, marriage, education, religion, values, economics, and politics—by learning about the lives of particular people.

Steps to Follow

1. Be certain that the goals of ethnographic research are clear in your mind. As with all ethnography, the researcher seeks to avoid imposing his or her *own* cultural interpretations and understandings but rather seeks to *discover* those meanings that are important to the culture under study. Ethnographic field work starts with what Spradley has termed a conscious attitude of ignorance.

2. Make arrangements to meet with your culture partner who will serve as a cultural informant. An informant is a person who shares information. I recommend you choose someone from a culture as different as possible from your own, about which you presently know nothing but which you would be interested in knowing about. I will pair you with a student from Inter-Link who has volunteered to be interviewed. Tell him/her the nature of your assignment and ask if he/she will let you interview him/her. Set up a time and place where you have privacy and an hour to an hour and a half of time for each of nine meetings.

3. Conduct *ethnographic* interviews. Ethnographic interviews consist of two parts: Grand Tours and Mini Tours. To get the details considered important by the informant, you first must ask for a grand tour. Let the informant be the guide who points out the important highlights. You can later return to the highlights mentioned by the informant and ask for a mini tour of each of these.

a. Grand Tour. To get the informant to give you the grand tour, ask him or her to tell you about his/her life as a child or ask him/her to tell you what it was like to grow up in his/her country. Write as much of what he/she says as possible, trying to write everything in *his/her words. Don't interrupt to ask questions.* If he/she asks you to guide him/her, tell him/her to share what seems important to himself/herself. Remind him/her that you don't know what features are important.

b. Mini Tour. After your informant completes the grand tour, you can ask him/her to go back to parts he/she mentioned and give you the mini tour of these, that is, to provide more detail. When you ask these, choose terms he/she used in his/her earlier grand tour and ask him/her to tell you more. This may take one or two follow-up meetings. It is possible to conduct mini tours within mini tours. Just remember that the questions you ask should be used to help elucidate or provide a more complete picture of the topics he/she has brought up. Avoid asking questons based on *your* categories of meaning.

4. Take thorough notes during the interview. It is important that you take down all information in the words of the informant. Do not try to summarize by putting things in your own words, or you may lose important meanings. Key phrases in the grand tour will be very useful for your coming back to the ideas in the mini tours. Exact wording is crucial to the analysis of the data which will be explained later.

5. Remember at all times to adhere to the ethical principles in anthropological research listed by Spradley.

TEACHER SOLUTIONS AND APPLICATIONS

Friday Lunches: A Program of Cross-Cultural Interaction

RICHARD ROBYN
Ashland College

One of the simplest, cheapest, and yet most effective of the international programs at Ashland College is the Friday Lunch Program started in October, 1980.

Dedicated to the idea that cross-cultural communication seems to work so much better over a meal, the program brings local elementary and secondary students together with foreign students on the college campus for a series of lunches and conversation. Since each series typically involves some 30 foreign students and twice that number of local pupils, and there are four series each year, there may be as many as 300 participants each academic year in this particular program of cross-cultural interaction.

The mechanics of the program are really quite simple. The participating American and foreign students are prepared with names and biographies of their partners and possible topics of discussion, brought together in the college cafeteria on a prearranged Friday, and paired off for an hour of lunch. Because of the reality of numbers and for ease of communication, there are typically two American kids for each foreign student. The same groups are then brought together at the same time for the next two Fridays so that there is a continuity to the developing relationships.

The local school pupils are organized by the coordinator of gifted programs with the Ashland City Schools, Mr. David Kowalka. This job involves locating interested teachers and pupils from grade six in the the seven local elementary schools or from the junior high school. Permission from parents and principals is then secured. "The response has been excellent," he reports, "Parents have been very cooperative, paying for the lunches and taking the time to bring their children to the cafeteria. Some even stay and take pictures." Teachers are encouraged to prepare their pupils for the interaction by having them write autobiographies for exchange, by doing some research on the countries of their partners, and by preparing questions about life in the foreign culture. There is pre- and post-program sharing of the experience in the classroom.

The cost of the lunch is paid by the participants. For the local school pupils, the parents pay. In case this poses a problem, the gifted program of the Ashland School System would pay. For those foreign students who are on the college meal plan, cost of the lunch is already included and no more payment is necessary. Those not on the meal plan are expected to pay. If this is a problem, the student is not required to eat, but may still participate in the program. Transportation of the school pupils is done by the buses of the school system. There are no transportation costs for the foreign student since the program is on campus. These are virtually the only costs associated with the program besides paper for occasional handouts.

Initially a voluntary activity for the foreign student, the Friday Lunch Program has proved of such pedagogical value that it has become a required part of the intermediate and advanced listening/speaking curriculum of the Ashland College Center for English Studies (AC'CESS), the campus IEP. Friday Lunch activities replace the regular listening/speaking class for that day, and there are pre- and post-lunch classroom activities to support the cross-cultural interaction. The character and number of these classroom activities will vary depending upon the linguistic level of the students and the familiarity they may have with the program from previous participation; however, the following schedule of activities excerpted from the program teacher's manual gives an indication of the possibilities:

1. First week of AC'CESS session (usually three weeks before first Friday Lunch encounter). Assignment: Write a 1-2 page autobiography, to be passed to the elementary school pupil. (Note: the autobiography can be done as a writing assignment in the writing class.)

2. Monday of the first Friday Lunch Program meeting (class time: 5-10 minutes). Teacher reminds students about the program, tells them that time in Thursday's class will be devoted to discussion/answering questions. If any immediate questions need to be answered at this time to relieve anxiety or misunderstandings, it may be wise to take the time to answer them now.

3. The class before the first meeting (class time: 5-20 minutes). Discussion and question/answer period. There may be some anxiety on the part of certain students, and this is a good time to offer suggestions and reassurance. Discussion can center around the following topics: the mechanics of the meeting (time, place, procedures), remembering that this is a series of three meetings all with the same pupil(s). Conversation topics: Usually conversation at the first meeting will center around introductions, family information, school life, etc. Students with previous Friday Lunch Program experience can help flesh out this part of the discussion. If the pupils' autobiographies are available, this would help in the discussion. Students may need to be reminded about the purpose of the program and how best to take advantage of the situation.

4. The class after the first Friday Lunch Program meeting (class time: 20-30 minutes). Discussion and question/answer period. The discussion can focus on topics brought up during lunch. This can be useful for everyone to hear, to compare notes, to generate ideas on topics. Students can describe their partners, their families; relate other information, the most unusual/funniest thing that happened, their reactions to the pupils, unusual vocabulary words, etc. If the teacher attended the Friday Lunch Program and picked up any particular problems in pronunciation, vocabulary, grammar, or topics, this could be a good time to bring them up and take care of them in a structured way. Students may need some time to ask questions or bring up any problems they may have encountered. Often, "veteran" students can help in answering the questions. Now is the time to remind students about the next meeting. Usually, realia is part of the second meeting—they can bring such things as stamps, coins, origami, postcards, pictures, traditional clothes, picture books, etc. Possible assignment: prepare a short presentation using realia, to present in class the day before the Friday Lunch Program.

5. The class before the second meeting (class time: 5-30 minutes). A reminder about the program and about realia. Offer a discussion about possible topics, problems. Students may or may not need a discussion; they may or may not make a realia presentation. Possible homework: report on partner realia.

6. The class after the second meeting (class time: 5-20 minutes). Depending on homework assignment, teacher/student interest in particular topics, or problems/breakthroughs, this discussion could be a short or long one. By this time, the partners are getting used to each other and so may not need a great deal of guidance or help. On the other hand, since they are getting used to each other and have probably touched on a great variety of topics, this could be a good time to explore certain topics in greater depth or new topics the students hadn't considered. Possible assignment: choose a topic, prepare series of questions, interview the partner, report back.

7. The class before the third meeting (class time: 5-10 minutes). A reminder about the third meeting. Students can bring cameras to this last meeting; they may also expect their partners to take their pictures. Students are also encouraged to take the addresses and phone numbers of their partners and to contact them during the break or anytime in the future. A discussion can be offered, short or long.

8. The class after the third meeting (class time: 5-10 minutes). A final period of discussion, short or long. A long discussion could center around what the students learned from this series of the Friday Lunch Program, a recapitulation of topics covered.

Conversation Topics: A Partial List
In any one discussion period, the teacher may not want to exploit the full range of topics available to the students in a conversation situation of the

kind offered by the Friday Lunch Program. Instead, picking and choosing from the following (partial) list of possible topics, the teacher can spread out these topics over the three weeks of the program:

1. **Introductions:** greetings, self-introduction, introducing a friend, steps in an initial conversation. Compare to introductions in their countries.

2. **School Life:** typical day, length of classes, subjects studied, favorite teacher (and why), size of class, facilities (gym, library, cafeteria, etc.), lunch (kinds of food, length of lunch period, cost), homework, study periods, extracurricular activities, differences between this year's grade level and last year's, the principal (description, what he does), attendance policy, textbook (can the pupil bring one to look at?), recess. Compare to school life in their countries.

3. **Play, Recreation:** vacations (describe, compare sites visited), favorite sport (to play and to watch), school parties, slumber parties, TV (how many hours/week, favorite shows and why, etc.), video games, sports heroes, rules of games/sports, typical weekend activities. Compare to sports/recreation in their countries.

4. **Friends:** boyfriends/girlfriends, what is a friend? how many friends should you have? what do friends do together? Compare concepts of friendships to those in their countries.

5. **Food:** favorite food, food at school, food at home, different food they have tried. Compare to food in their countries.

6. **Jokes:** tell a joke, practical jokes, riddles, puns. Tell a joke from their culture.

7. **Family Life:** size of family, brother and sisters (ages and descriptions), father (description, occupation), mother (description, occupation), grandparents (description, where they live, how often visit), chores, pets, rules of the house, description of the house. Compare to family life in their countries.

8. **Growing up in Ashland:** How long have the pupils lived in Ashland, fun things to do here. (Make a list: this can help the foreign student discover the town, nearby sites.)

9. **Future:** what do they want to be when they grow up (and why), looking forward to junior high or high school (differences from sixth grade, teachers they have heard about, subjects, extra-curricular activities). Compare to their own future goals.

The program has benefited both international and elementary/secondary student programming in a variety of ways. The cultural interchange has been an obvious benefit: the American pupils, some of whom have never traveled outside of Ohio, learn about foreign countries and customs firsthand, and have the opportunity for an extended conversation with a person whose national language is not English. The international students have a chance to learn about the lives of young Americans, a group too often not met or heard from in their stay in America. They have the opportunity to practice English in a structured yet informal setting, with a "real" (i.e., not a professional educator) American. This creates an unusual listening situation: a

110

different method of speaking, strange accents, new vocabulary, all taking place in a "real" (noisy) setting. The opportunity is there to practice structures, pronunciation, vocabulary, conversation strategies, and topics learned in the classroom or to learn and explore new ones not covered in the class. The cross-cultural interaction that takes place provides an opportunity to learn about aspects of American life too often missed in textbooks or in the typical college foreign student experience: elementary school life, family life, play and recreation, food, growing up in Ashland and in America, and many more.

Besides linguistic or cultural benefits, positive attitudinal changes can occur. For the bold student, aided by a sympathetic teacher, the program can offer a release from the classroom, a chance to explore entirely new areas in his education. For the timid student, also supported by the teacher, there is the challenge of overcoming shyness, of learning self-reliance in conversations, of putting newly learned patterns into practice. Potential attitudinal changes may include a greater self-confidence, higher self-esteem, a brighter outlook on American life and customs, and a more positive feeling about English mastered and towards education in AC'CESS.

There are other benefits that have come as a result of the program's operation that, while welcome, are not central to the program itself. Students tell of friendships begun, sometimes of host family invitations, and pen-pal exchanges. One Venezuelan student, casually remarking on an upcoming birthday, was surprised by an invitation to the elementary school for a party in his honor. An increased interest in language learning has been another result: for the foreign students, learning and practicing casual conversational English; for the elementary pupils, an increased enrollment in foreign language classes. Publicity has also been one result: the local newspaper published prominently a picture of a Kuwaiti student at a lunch showing his country's money to two American pupils.

While providing many benefits, the program also presents problems at certain times for some foreign students. It is not always easy to carry off an hour's conversation with a stranger from a foreign country who is not your own age. Feelings of anxiety, boredom, frustration, and fatigue can surface. Teachers and program administrators need to be aware of this so that these normal reactions do not get out of hand.

Perhaps the best way to deal with this is for everyone involved with the program to recognize that putting the proper perspective on feelings is a major task for persons, and especially young persons, in a cross-cultural situation. Presenting challenging situations that may arouse a range of feelings from fear of the unknown to impatience with repetition can provide catalysts to help students not only learn key points of knowledge about others, but also learn about themselves as well: their strengths and weaknesses, and what they need to do to succeed in a certain place and time. If we and our students accept that, then any "problem" that comes up is in reality only a "challenge" to overcome.

A Fusion of Traditions: Family Folklore as a New Method for Teaching Composition within Intensive English Programs

EVE CECH
University of Florida

Composition teachers generally agree that students should have some personal interest in and knowledge of the subjects they are asked to write about. This need is especially crucial for the foreign student who is faced both with learning the target language—English—and with managing an intelligent development of a topic he may or may not know anything about, while at the same time learning how to interact within the context of a new cultural experience. As many of us have discovered, it is quite difficult to select composition topics for foreign students that will draw on their existing knowledge, be personally meaningful, acknowledge the cross-cultural bridges the students are constructing, and also be suitable for sustained writing in English.

But subjects based on the personal and cultural experience of the writer are inherently meaningful, and some composition theorists (Macrorie and Elbow for instances) argue that such a personal involvement between writers and their material is indispensable to the writing process. In addition to addressing the writing process itself, the emphasis on writing topics that deal with personal experience gives the students a chance to be an authority on a subject in an environment where they (in this case foreign students) daily confront the shortcomings of their expertise in our language and culture, and where the required interaction with a new culture and its language can be overwhelming, frustrating, and, at times, resented. As we know, some foreign students will resist and defend against totally immersing themselves in a new language and its culture because such an interaction implies for them, either

113

literally or unconsciously, the loss of their own cultural identity and language. As Stevick (1980) observes, "the preservation of the self-image is the first law of psychological survival."

By stressing assignments of a personal nature, this basic cultural and psychological struggle can be significantly eased. With these considerations in mind, I have developed a writing course and a general approach to teaching composition within intensive English programs that stress cross-cultural communication by drawing their subject matter from the life and heritage of the individual students, their families, their cultures, their traditions. Central to this course is a book of family folklore which the students create and which relates the history and folklore of their families by means of a series of writing assignments, including narratives involving family members and their biographies, definitions of family customs, process descriptions of family activities, and the like.

By "family folklore book", I mean an actual, illustrated book, written and designed by students to document their family history, family traditions, and family lore. (Francelia Butler, professor of English at the University of Connecticut, uses the family folklore book in her undergraduate English courses. I am indebted to her for providing the basic model for this kind of assignment.) In the announcement for the Smithsonian Institution's recent touring exhibition of family folklore, Amy Kotkin, the curator of the exhibit, defines "family folklore" as a collection of "stories, traditions, customs, expressions, and artifacts that represent the creative ways in which families preserve their shared experiences. Family folklore represents the larger panorama of life and as such is a valuable source of social and political history." (This statement appeared in the general announcement sent to museums concerning the Touring Smithsonian Institution's Family Folklore Program. For additional information contact the Family Folklore Program, Smithsonian Institution, Washington, D.C.)

The writing of a family folklore book or its alternative project provides a rich source of lessons concerning such grammatical items as the use of appropriate narrative tenses, correct pronoun references, parallel sentence structures, punctuation rules, and the myriad other elements which comprise clear, effective writing. However, I first applied the folklore book to the teaching of ESL composition because I felt that, however imperfectly written it might be, the process of creating such a book was an exercise in the essence of communication. Stevick (1976), among others, argues for the importance of creating a meaningful context for learning and for memory retention, one in which a student is able to communicate freely, without feelings of self-consciousness or inadequacy. Thus, in the writing of the folklore book, the students write about the values and achievements, and sometimes the struggles and limitations, of the lives that shaped theirs. Often the students recount these family stories with subtlety, dignity, and poetic power. For example, one student wrote about the heroic exploits of an older brother who had brought "fragrance" to the family name; another poignantly recalled her

114

father's account of being sold into slavery as a young child in Java; and a Mexican student wrote about a widowed mother who singlehandedly reared and educated six children. In the process of evoking a family story—some of them powerfully moving, some hilarious, some quite ordinary—the student learns an indispensable lesson in the target language—how to create a narrative voice in it.

For those students who feel that the subjects involved in writing a family history are too sensitive or too personal to share with an entire class, I have devised the "Cultural Calendar of Events" as an alternative assignment to the "Family Folklore Book." The cultural calendar asks the students to research and write about more general topics in the folklore of their cultures without necessarily focusing on the writer's family. See Part II of the Appendix for a list of some of the subjects that can be included in the cultural calendar.

Ultimately, the teaching of English composition via a family folklore book calls for the use of the English langauge as well as the evocation of the personal voice of the writer. And it is the discovery of this personal voice that Macrorie (1970) identifies as the central task in teaching American students how to write. Moreover, the family folklore book not only provides a context for teaching the elements of written discourse to foreign students, but it does so while preserving the students' dignity and identity while they are finding a new voice in a new language. In the process of this development, the students contribute to their teacher's and their fellow students' understanding of this personal and cultural identity. It has been my experience that when students discuss and critique each other's work in the course of writing their family histories, they undergo what Peter Elbow (1973) considers to be an essential part of the writing process: they teach themselves and each other about writing clearly and effectively. Furthermore, when the students present their books to the class as a whole at the end of the course, these personal expressions have built bonds of understanding and tolerance between students who may have begun the course as cultural antagonists. For example, when an Arab student discovered that he shared with his Latin American classmate the same proverbial wisdom about not "awakening" potentially volatile situations ("Let sleeping dogs lie"), they suddenly found they had something to talk about together. English, then, becomes the common meeting ground for different cultures, families, and personalities—the place where people meet other people in the process of communicating something very important about themselves to one another, in a voice that is both comprehensible and unique.

Having provided this introduction, this *raison d'etre* for such an approach, let me explain in specific terms the method I have adopted for teaching composition through the vehicle of the family folklore book.

On the first day of the assignment, I hand out copies of the Folklore Project Outline (Appendix). We discuss the two possible projects—the family folklore book and the cultural calendar of events—and add to the list of topics in the outline. The students choose one of the projects, and they are then asked to prepare an outline for it. In the case of the family folklore book, the outline consists of the names of family members (three generations), which are later presented in the book itself as a family tree. Next, the students are asked to select several family members about whom they will write individual biographical sketches. Finally, students choose other topics from the outline for the text of their folklore book. The students discuss their outlines with the instructor, augmenting and rearranging them when necessary, and then using them as the tables of contents for the books they will be writing.

After the introduction of the folklore book assignment, the class begins its study of the six forms of written English discourse (narrative, definition, process, cause and effect, comparison and contrast, and classification), fusing the knowledge of these formal English structures with the content of family or cultural lore. Much as in a traditional English composition class in which grammar, logic, and rhetoric are the major concerns, considerable time is spent discussing and analyzing the purpose, grammar, organizaton, and style of the given form (Corbett 1971). For instance, if I were to assign students a definition composition, I might ask them to define a proverb, noting that they should begin their discussion with a thesis statement (an essential idea that is, of course, applied in teaching each of the composition forms). I would then ask them to give an example of a proverb from their households and explain it, since many proverbs do not translate from one language into another. Finally, I would ask them to comment on the general validity of the proverb based on their experience and observations of life. In reading this composition, I would again look for all the traditional marks of good writing— a logical organization with clearly presented ideas, interesting and pertinent examples, and a lucid writing style. Working with my comments as well as those of other students in the class, the writer would then revise the composition, repeating the process as necessary. As composition teachers we know that the process of revision is arduous enough for readers working in their native language, but the possibilities for frustration are compounded for someone who is writing in a new language. However, this process often becomes a challenging, exciting endeavor with the family folklore book because here the students are writing about people and matters that are extremely important to them. Indeed, the only "problem" that I have encountered with revisions of the folklore book assignments is that the students find that they have much more to say than the medium (or the semester) permits.

I follow essentially the same procedure in teaching the remaining composition forms, making each of these forms relevant to our central purpose— writing the folklore book. In addition to helping the students select a topic for writing, the instructor will need to integrate lessons about pertinent points of grammar, organization, and rhetorical elements with the particular composition form being taught. Thus, for example, when teaching the process composition form in which students describe such activities as how to tap a rubber tree, how to repair a piece of pottery, or how to arrange a marriage, the instructor will also need to present and explain the uses of active and passive voice constructions, imperative sentences, and the need for establish-

116

ing a chronological order of events. In short, while the subject matter centers on family and cultural folklore, the basic instruction is the same as it would be for any composition course. During the course of preparing these compositions, especially as the students are reading and critiquing one another's works, they discover at first hand the necessity for these formal composition rules.

The family folklore book offers the student a rich variety of assignment possibilities, all of which are close to his experience and all of which also give him valuable practice in using and understanding the standard forms of English composition. For example, a comparison/contrast assignment can be based on a discussion of the character differences between two family members or by contrasting solemn and joyous family holidays. A cause-and-effect composition could deal with a traditional family value that has significantly influenced the student's life. A classification composition can be based on a description of the various stages of life that occur within a student's family and culture, drawing on the student's family members as the illustrations for each of these life passages. Or, a student could classify the kinds of occupations, amusements, houses, or dress of three generations of family members. These are just a sampling of the kinds of assignments that can be generated. The students themselves, I have found, will provide many additional ideas for their writing. Many will be eager to illustrate their written assignments with drawings, photographs, calligraphy, and other graphics, and at times will incorporate actual artifacts, such as a cherished piece of family lace, a small carving, or other important mementos.

The obvious academic benefit to the students doing the family folklore books is that they learn and hone their composition and research skills. Often a student will need to establish a correspondence with various family members to collect the necessary information about his or her family. Frequently, students may have to do research in the library about their cultures to find and learn the English vocabulary to write about them. In the personal realm, the benefits are equally significant. For in the process of creating the family folklore book, the students establish themselves in a generational continuum; they create a valuable family document; they become spokespersons for their cultures, building a bridge of understanding between themselves, students from other cultures, and the teacher. As you know, teaching composition is difficult, but with the family folklore book, this process becomes, for both teacher and student, an exciting, deeply rewarding experience in which the students can discover their voices, and you, the teacher, get the distinct pleasure of hearing them.

Appendix

I. Family Folklore Project Outline
1. A family tree
2. The history of how your family came to settle where it did
3. How your family got its name
4. Stories or anecdotes about your family members, interesting, unusual or famous individuals. Unusual experiences of family members.
5. Proverbs which are spoken in your family, especially by grandparents and other older members of your family
6. Superstitions that are told in your family
7. Songs, poems, or tales that are handed down by family members
8. Games that are played by family members
9. Traditional jobs or work that your family is known for
10. Family rituals and celebrations—marriages, births, deaths, etc.
11. Recipes—include occasions when the foods are served
12. Family property—land, farms, houses, businesses, factories, etc.
13. Family heirlooms
14. Family values—discipline practices, rewards for accomplishments, particular virtues

Please note: Use family photos, illustrations, or drawings to illustrate your books!

II: Cultural Calendar of Events
1. Discuss events in your country and region during the year
2. Decide on seasonal or monthly calendar
3. Include some of the following information
   a. Stories associated with months or seasons
   b. Rituals, celebrations, and festivals
   c. Songs
   d. Games
   e. Foods associated with seasons
   f. Jokes and riddles
   g. Weather lore (stories about the seasons)
   h. Social customs—when do marriages usually take place? when does school begin?
4. Children—general stories, stories about school, holidays, customs or events that honor children
5. Teenagers—apply the same questions as you would to the section on children
6. Family—apply the same questions as you would to the section on children

Remember that the senses of sight, sound, touch, taste, and smell will help to remember events from your life and your culture.

TEACHER SOLUTIONS AND APPLICATIONS

Peer Telephoning Promotes Interaction and Harmony

CAROL HARMATZ-LEVIN
Georgetown University

One of the most unpredictable factors in trying to establish a productive mood in a language classroom is the way in which students will get along with each other. Teachers can facilitate a relaxed, non-threatening atmosphere in a variety of ways—with their personal styles of behavior, communicative exercises, and circular seating arrangements.

The potential for tension, nonetheless, is very much a reality in many ESL classrooms. Negative attitudes, stemming from a number of factors, may be harbored by many of the students. First, there are feelings of insecurity that arise from linguistic adjustments that students have to make. For perhaps the first time in their lives, students are unable to express themselves. Many of them are successful achievers; some are accomplished professionals, and now they are reduced to feeling child-like and inadequate. Even with years of secondary school English behind them, students must now perform under the stress of perhaps an intensive program of language study, or at least a program in which they are expected to do more than sit back and absorb. Second, there is culture shock. Adjustments need to be made to being in a foreign country and to being in a classroom—possibly after a long absence from it. Being away from one's family and friends may also exacerbate adjustment problems, as well as a new climate, new food, and the myriad of stimuli encountered in daily living. Third, being in a classroom that is multicultural adds further possibilities for tension. Since this may be the first time many students find themselves faced with other foreign nationals, they may need to deal with stereotypical expectations of others' behavior as well as the way other students perceive them. The political issues between Taiwanese and mainland Chinese, between Arabs and Israelis, and between Koreans and Japanese surface in ESL classrooms.

With all of this potential for tension, focusing on the group as a learning unit becomes increasingly difficult. The group, however, is a key to successful classroom interaction. If the students are in an interactive situation, there is no alternative other than facing the group daily. Language is, after all, an interactive skill; it cannot be internalized if students feel isolated from or, at worst, antagonized by fellow students. Earl Stevick (1976) has underscored the importance of providing a learning situation in which students need not be defensive, but rather, receptive. Furthermore, the focus of classroom teaching needs to be shifted from the teacher as the giver of information. Students need to serve as active language models for each other; as a group, they need to support and correct each other and take responsibility for their learning.

Getting students to invest themselves in the learning they have undertaken is the issue I needed to address when teaching a small group of adult EFL students in a twenty-hour-a-week university program. In the third week of a seven-week session, the problem was made apparent by the inconsistency with which homework was being prepared, the lack of enthusiasm for doing group or pair work, and the quiet, unsocial break times. The class was not functioning well as a group. Certain students did not work effectively when placed in the same small group, and random grouping consistently resulted in problems. Therefore, as part of my lesson planning, I set up small group work carefully and took into account nationality, language background, personality conflicts, and language proficiency.

When I was announcing my divisions one day, a usually cooperative student solemnly looked at me and shook his head. I had obviously not made the correct choice of partner for him. I was so tired of juggling that I didn't respond immediately, but another student noticed the impending disaster in those few seconds. She abandoned her partner, grabbed the unwanted match and sat down.

The problem was solved, but later in the class period when only half of the students had prepared homework, I knew that I had to modify my classroom management procedures. At this point, I set up a system of telephoning for the class. On the board I wrote each student's name, phone number, and a period of time when they chose to be available to speak on the telephone. It was difficult to pin some students down, but waking and retiring hours provided guidelines. As a homework assignment, each student was to call two others, one of whom did not speak the same native language. Students asked me what they had to talk about; I said that it didn't matter. In fact, I only wanted them to make contact.

The next day I recorded the names of who had initiated calls to whom. I did not reprimand those who had not called or who had made only one, and I accepted attempts which yielded only a busy signal. I made the same assignment on three consecutive days and once more a week later.

During this time several remarkable things happened. First, there was considerable chatter when I entered the classroom on the following day. A male Saudi student who had called a Venezuelan woman had had to deal with her young daughters first. Not only was there healthy giggling and oral language practice in the few minutes before class, but the Saudi was excited about getting to know a classmate's family. A one-dimensional relationship had become more human.

Second, all of the students participated in the assignment actively. Those who had not called anyone on the first night initiated two and sometimes three calls on the next two nights. Furthermore, students did not call the same classmates repeatedly. Classmates from a wide cross-section of language backgrounds were approached; friendly, safe students were called as were the quiet and the aggressive ones. By the third night, much to my surprise, the student who had refused to work in the pair I had arranged for him actually called the classmate he had rejected; on the next day, the gesture was returned. After three nights of assigned telephoning, nearly half of the class continued the activity on their own on the fourth night.

What I had at first considered a whimsical idea was, in fact, the push that these students needed to break the tension that had been inhibiting their success as a group. Linguistically, they were encouraged to practice their new skills outside the classroom. Those who felt inhibited by being in a classroom were exposed to a task that extended learning beyond the sometimes confining four walls. The assignment was challenging, and yet, since it was done on a peer level without teacher evaluation, it was not threatening. Various human-istic needs were fulfilled as well, and as a result, adjustment to a new situation eased. Students began to view each other as multifaceted human beings, and cultural stereotypes became less rigid. Above all, the absence of family and friends in the United States was eased, if even just a little, by the awareness that classmates could care about classmates.

TEACHER SOLUTIONS AND APPLICATIONS

Cultural Assumptions, Frames, and the Allowable Economies of English: A Cross-Cultural Problem

SALLY STODDARD
University of Nebraska-Lincoln

Members of every cultural group share a common knowledge based on the defining characteristics of the community. If a member of a particular group, in speaking or writing which is addressed to fellow members, makes this information explicit, it is redundant. To avoid this redundancy, the information is made implicit or simply taken for granted. The importance of this for persons from another cultural group (such as foreign college students in the United States) is that they are excluded from fully understanding what they read or hear. For these students, reading textbooks and listening to conversations and lectures can be frustrating because they do not have enough cultural knowledge to adequately infer the information which is implicit. Because the problem is greatest for written English where students cannot ask for clarification from the writer, this paper addresses a change in approach to reading. (Writing is also involved, but the implications are too extensive to consider here.)

Basically, implicit cultural assumptions are a cognitive problem. That is, what is not explicit may be non-interpretable to non-native speakers because they have not acquired appropriate knowledge frames (Minsky 1975) for particular aspects of the unfamiliar culture, or the knowledge frames they do have are inadquate. Some examples of written English texts will illustrate this point. Harper Lee in setting the scene in *To Kill a Mockingbird* says, "Maycomb County had recently been told that it had nothing to fear but fear itself." The unstated agent for the passive verb <u>had been told</u> is "Franklin Roosevelt," which is common knowledge to Americans, but not to foreign students. That is, their frame of knowledge based on their experience is inadequate to

123

interpret the agentless verb. In this case, the interpretation is critical to placing the story in the 1930s. Likewise, Eric Sevareid in *This is Eric Sevareid* speaks of hearing the "shriek of brakes, the heavy throbbing of the one-a-day Braniff airliner into Monet, the shattering sirens born of war. . . ." The interpretation of these definite noun phrases depends on knowledge frames of the United States (i.e., on referents that are not explicit prior to that point in the text), knowledge which foreign students could not be expected to have acquired.

Grammatical structures (such as those above) allow the reduction of what the writers assumed to be cultural "givens." These structures are chosen for their stylistic effects on a native speaker audience. Stylistic economy of explicit information is possible because of deletions and/or substitutions, as when the agents of verbals and of passive verbs are deleted from a text; or when "definite" noun phrases are substituted for their frame node; or when pronouns are used with or without explicit referents. However, even a good understanding of these grammatical structures will not solve the non-native speaker's confusion because deletion and substitution also result from employing metaphorical extensions and various lexical choices. In sum, then, knowledge frames, grammatical structures, and lexical devices work together to reduce redundancy for native speakers of English even though the process increases the task of interpretation for ESL students. Clearly, ESL students need to understand the nature of the problem and to learn different strategies for coping with it in order to avoid continual feelings of inadequacy.

A sound approach to modifying the reading strategies of our students will point out to them the fact that much that is written in English is understood, not because it is physically in the written text, but because readers bring certain kinds of knowledge to the interpretation process. In other words, our students need to understand the importance of what is *not* stated, as well as what *is* stated, to better comprehend what they read. The method described here concentrates on inferential strategies to "bridge inferential gaps" (Clark 1975). This means students must develop their powers of inferring from explicit data given in the text. (Lawrence 1972 has invaluable suggestions for getting students started in the process.) Here, knowledge frames are used as vehicles for more sophisticated inferencing. Where students already have established frames, the frames may be inadequate and need fleshing out; where they do not have appropriate knowledge frames, of course, appropriate frames need to be established.

In order to understand how knowledge frames operate, a lesson may start by asking students to simply list everything that comes to their minds when they are presented with a cultural phenomenon such as "shopping center." In any given class, the students' knowledge of that which suburban dwellers in the United States take for granted will vary in kind and generally will be quite limited (and some of it may be misperceptions). For the knowledge frame node "shopping center," the student might list such things as: paved parking lot, small stores, food stores, shoppers, gas station, barbershop, bank, cars, and so on. (These lists rarely will be as sophisticated as those of American students whose experiences of shopping centers may trigger such additional items, perhaps, as: sidewalk sales, midway rides in summer, Santa Claus at Christmas, teenagers' hangouts, Coke machines, specific kinds of stores, and so on.)

The next step is to take the shopping center frame and put it into a context from literature, such as Loren Eiseley's essay, "The Brown Wasps," where the following sentence appears:

> One day as I cut across the field which at that time extended on one side of our suburban shopping center, I found a giant slug feeding from a runnel of pink ice cream in an abandoned Dixie cup.

Here, the context presents the frame "shopping center" in a setting which probably is not at all familiar to ESL students because they have not lived in this country long enough to watch a suburban development evolve. If students again make lists of all the features that interface with the shopping center frame, they will need to use their powers of inference. In so doing, they will need to push their thinking beyond the obvious. Some questions suggested by the teacher may help them in this process. When did this happen? What was the writer doing? Why was the writer cutting across? What has happened to the field? How do we know that something has changed in regard to the field? Why does the writer say "our shopping center"? Why would a giant slug be found there? What season of the year was it? How do you know? What do you suppose a "Dixie cup" is? Where was the cup? What do you suppose a "runnel" is? Why was the ice cream pink? Why were the cup and ice cream there? And so on. The questions direct the students' attention to the relationship and interaction of the various frames and subframes. Once students fill in the gaps in the information, a whole scenario begins to evolve, and they realize that much of what they thought they "didn't know" they really do know or are able to interpret logically.

This technique can be applied to readings for ESL classes (such as those in Johnson 1983) or to textbooks in classes which are likely to have cultural bases (e.g., political science, art history, geography of the United States). Learning to do the kind of thinking required to bridge inferential gaps can affect foreign students in several positive ways. First, they will understand why some parts of the texts they read do not always make sense. This understanding will reassure them that their basic intelligence is not at fault; rather, it is their lack of appropriate reading strategies. Second, they will, with practice, be better able to cope with cultural gaps as they arise and to minimize the lapses. Third, they will have increased their powers of inferring from all kinds of input data. Finally, our students will gain a greater appreciation for the nuances of another culture.

The Fear of Speaking: Communication Anxiety in ESL Students

ARMEDA C. REITZEL
Humboldt State University

High motivation and positive self-esteem contribute to the learning of a second language, but a high level of anxiety may inhibit second language acquisition (Krashen 1981). Foreign ESL students who are highly communicative in their own languages and cultures may become so anxious during speaking situations in English that they become physically tense and emotionally reluctant to communicate. Intensive English program teachers need to understand the phenomenon of communication anxiety in ESL students and know of ways to deal with this problem.

This article discusses the fear of speaking that many ESL students experience. First, communication anxiety is defined. Second, the ways in which communication anxiety may affect ESL students are explained. Third, strategies for helping ESL students overcome their fear of speaking are described.

Communication anxiety refers to the level of apprehension, in regard to communicative interaction, that is so intense and powerful ". . . that it becomes debilitative, inhibiting effective self-expression" (Adler and Rodman 1985:310). Some anxiety about speaking situations is natural for native speakers of English as well as for nonnative speakers of English. The term "communication anxiety" is used by communication scholars to indicate levels of fear which are abnormally high and lead to physical and emotional turmoil. In order to avoid such turmoil, those suffering from communication anxiety may withdraw from or refuse to enter into communication situations.

A major factor contributing to communication anxiety among ESL students is culture shock, the "occupational disease of people who have been suddenly transplanted abroad" (Oberg 1979:43). Many foreigners experience what may be called the "everything is awful stage" of culture shock (Dodd 1982:99–101). The familiar signs and patterns of verbal and nonverbal behavior are different in or absent from the new culture. ESL students might become confused or misunderstand what native speakers are saying. The students might inadvertently offend native speakers by the inappropriate use of non-verbal or verbal cues. Such confusion may cause anxiety.

The result of high levels of anxiety is "cultural fatigue" (Donahue and Heyde-Parsons 1982). "Fatigue is a natural result of such a continued state of alertness" (Barna 1982:329). Foreign students may become emotionally and physically exhausted due to the "infinite series of minute adjustments they must make in the new culture" (Szanston 1966:48). This exhaustion could result in a "withdrawal" or "fleeing" reaction in which the foreign students avoid speaking the second language and interacting with native speakers. Such a reaction slows down the process of learning English.

Intensive English program teachers can help their students overcome communication anxiety so that their progress in learning English does not come to a standstill, a situation which could lead to further anxiety. The remainder of this article describes some approaches that ESL teachers can use in their classrooms. These approaches are (1) educating the students about culture shock, (2) using modeling in the classroom, (3) working through a communication anxiety hierarchy, and (4) using oral interpretation and drama in the classroom.

The first recommended strategy is to educate ESL students about the common phenomenon of culture shock. Even highly motivated students may go through a period of cultural conflict, the "everything is awful stage." No matter how much reading a foreign student may have done about the host country, he/she will not know about all the nuances of meaning possible in the host country's patterns of verbal and nonverbal communication. He/she will not know about all the cultural values and assumptions that he/she will encounter when interacting with host nationals. Students can better cope with their physical, emotional, and psychological conflicts and exhaustion if they understand what culture shock is, can identify its various stages and symptoms, and know how to deal with it. By knowing what they are experiencing, students will have an easier time handling the ambiguities of inter-cultural communication. Understanding the source of stress can help students learn the skills which will enable them to cope with culture shock and communication anxiety.

The second strategy is the use of modeling to develop the students' skills in recognizing and in using the communication patterns of the host country. Models can give students images of interactional behavior that they can imitate in the classroom and later use "in the field." The students could watch films and videotapes of native speakers in various situations. Videotapes of media interviews, situation comedies, and even soap operas contain a wealth of information about communication patterns. After watching the models, the students could role play similar situations. These role-playing sessions

128

could be videotaped so that the students could compare their actions with those of the model. The rationale behind the use of modeling is to clear up some of the "unknowns" of interacting in a new culture.

Another approach to demystifying some of the mystery of the new culture is the third suggested strategy: working through a communication anxiety hierarchy. Teachers devise a sequence of communication situations which range from slightly stressful events, such as ordering a hamburger at a fast-food restaurant, to increasingly more stressful situations, such as giving a speech about one's country to a community organization. Each situation in the hierarchy is dealt with one at a time, starting with the least stressful event. Students read and practice dialogues which reflect how to handle the interactions typically found in that situation. After the students are familiar with the communication patterns called for, they write and practice their own dialogues. They receive feedback from classmates and their instructors. The final step is to place the students in an actual situation where they have to use what they have been studying. For example, the students could actually go to a fast-food restaurant to order their meals. This could be a class outing so that the students have peer and teacher support. By practicing the situation, the students should feel comfortable, and their anxiety about the interaction should not be debilitating. After the first situation is successfully completed, the students go on to the next situation in the hierarchy.

A fourth approach to helping students overcome their communication anxiety is the use of oral interpretation and drama. Oral interpretation involves the practiced oral reading of a piece of literature. The students have the opportunity to work on pronunciation, practice intonation patterns, and develop a general ease in speaking in a non-threatening atmosphere (Russo 1983). Drama is useful in teaching interpersonal and small group communication patterns in the host country. The skills learned through oral interpretation and drama can be transferred to everyday situations outside the classroom setting.

Communication anxiety is a phenomenon which many foreign students experience and, because of its debilitating effects, should be dealt with in the intensive English program classroom. ESL teachers can help their students overcome their fear of speaking in English by educating them about the phenomenon of culture shock and by teaching them interactional skills through a variety of experiential approaches. Language learning can be enhanced as the students' anxieties are lowered to more natural levels.

Conducting Research in the Community: Fine Tuning Language Skills While Learning American Culture

LYNNE ACKERBERG AND ELLEN D. COMER
Macalester College

Although the goal of most intensive ESL programs is to improve students' fluency in English, we believe that this is not sufficient to enable foreign students to compete successfully in an American undergraduate program. Our work has shown us that the language-learning experience should be combined with explicit cultural instruction designed to provide the students with specific information about life in the United States and to increase their understanding of American values and behavior. Foreign students are often at a disadvantage in American classrooms because, by virtue of their being foreign, they do not possess the same cultural references as the American students. The addition of a cultural component to the regular ESL program aids the students' adjustment process while simultaneously providing a very natural opportunity for language practice.

Within a course on American culture it is extremely important to provide the students with balanced views on the United States and to allow the students ample opportunities to test the validity of the generalizations made in class. An assignment which allows students to test their assumptions about a particular aspect of American culture and to show their ability to function in the English language is an original research project conducted by each student on some facet of contemporary American life.

Specifically, students are asked to prepare an oral and written report over a two-month period on an aspect of American culture which they wish to explore in detail. They are asked to synthesize information gathered from a variety of sources. For advanced level students, these sources come from the library and the college community as well as from the Minneapolis/St. Paul area. Intermediate students are not required to use sources from the library. This project provides an opportunity for students to test the validity of the information taught in class, to develop the skills needed to locate, organize, and synthesize information accumulated from a wide range of sources including interviews, and also to become better acquainted with the Twin Cities.

Early in the semester we present the goals of the project and a series of due dates and specifications for the final report. Then students choose and narrow their topics and form the preliminary questions they intend to answer. In small groups, they present their topics and questions. This group process helps generate additional questions, clarify questions, and provide a real audience for the student researcher. With a specific audience in mind students are more likely to be concise and clear.

With a preliminary topic decided upon, the next step is to gather resources. Finding resources in the community is not a very difficult task. People contacted by our students generally agree to the interviews and enjoy the experience. Following are some examples of community resources:

1. **Teachers and students' friends, acquaintances, and relatives:** This is the richest source.

2. **Members of the school or college community.** Interviewing faculty and staff has the added benefit of acquainting students with the culture of the school.

3. **Alumni files.** Alumni offices of many schools and colleges maintain lists of alumni willing to serve as resources to students.

4. **Public school community resource files.** Public schools also maintain lists of community resources.

5. **Newspaper announcements.** Local newspapers regularly announce speakers on a wide range of topics. We continually clip and file names and affiliations of resources.

6. **Representatives of the city, county, and state governmental agencies, special interest groups, and the media** have been willing to be interviewed by our students.

We find that students are highly motivated to practice language activities which will prepare them for successful interviewing. Moreover, interesting cross-cultural discussion about appropriate social behavior occurs as students anticipate conducting the interviews.

Language functions related to setting up, conducting or following up on interviews are suggested in the Appendix, Information Interviews. The amount and kind of preparation students need in order to conduct effective interviews will, of course, vary with the needs of the group.

In order to successfully set up an interview, students may benefit from practicing introducing themselves on the phone, giving directions to the college, and setting up or changing appointments. To conduct successful interviews, students may need practice paraphrasing questions in case the interviewee does not understand the questions, changing the topic, asking for additional information, or asking follow-up questions. Sources of such exercises are included in the Reference Section. (See Akiyama 1981; Lee 1983; Keller and Warner 1980a, 1980b; Jones and von Baeyer 1984.)

Questions arise related to appropriate social behavior when interviewing. Students are concerned about what kinds of questions are polite and which should be avoided; what topics are appropriate for small talk; how long small talk should continue; how the interviewee should be addressed, especially if the person is older; where an appropriate meeting place might be; who pays for coffee if the meeting takes place in a restaurant; and finally, whether the person should be sent a gift in appreciation for the interview.

Students benefit from conducting practice interviews and from role-playing difficult interview situations. Here are some sample situations: (1) an interviewee rambles on in response to simple questions, (2) An interviewee takes control of the interview, asking questions instead of responding to them, or (3) an interviewee answers questions in single-word answers. We have also prepared an interview on videotape which students analyze, pointing out the strengths of the interviewer and suggesting ways the interviewer could be more effective.

An important step in any research process is evaluating the credibility of the sources. In this project as well, students should become aware of the biases of the people they interview and the extent to which these biases color their data.

The form of the final report will depend on the students' level and the language skills emphasized in the class. Our course on the intermediate level emphasizes listening, speaking, and writing, so our students both write up their results and present them orally to the class. Advanced level students research their topics in the library, consulting traditional sources such as books and periodicals. Both intermediate and advanced level students present oral reports first. Then, responding to feedback from the class and teacher, they write a first draft. Finally, after discussion with the teacher, students write a final draft.

Students were actively involved in these projects and generally produced high quality reports on a variety of topics such as: The Great Depression: How It Affected Minnesotans; The Life and Problems of Vietnamese Refugees in the Twin Cities; Cross-Cultural Marriage; and The Role of Sports for Women. The contacts in the community which students established while doing this project provided them with an opportunity to confirm, modify, or refute assumptions that they held about an aspect of American culture and to test what they had learned from their texts and teachers. In addition, the entire process of preparing for and conducting interviews and reporting their findings provided a natural opportunity for students to use English.

Appendix
Handout on Information Interviews Given to Students
Prepared by Nancy Tellett-Royce, Career Development Center, Macalester College

Information Interviews

An information interview gives you a chance to gather information from someone. Many people are very willing to be interviewed. There are several steps you can take to be sure that your interview is successful for you and the person you interview.

Setting up the Interview.
1. Ask for an interview. Write out what you want to say.
   a. Introduce yourself.
   b. Briefly explain your project.
   c. Mention the name of someone who sent you.
   d. Tell how long you expect the interview to take.
   e. Arrange a time. Suggest several times that you will be available.
   f. Arrange a place. Be sure you know where you will be meeting. Take down the address and ask for directions if you are not sure how to get there. You may decide to do your interview by telephone. If so, arrange a time to call them that will be convenient.

   Example: Hello, _____, my name is _____. I am a student at Macalester. Your name was given to me by _____ at the Macalester Alumni Association. I am taking a course called _____, and one of my assignments is to do an information interview. Would you be willing to meet with me for about _____ minutes? I would like to talk with you about _____.

At the Interview
1. Introduce yourself again.
2. Shake hands.
3. Chat for a few minutes about the weather or getting to the interview.
4. Introduce your project again.
5. Ask the person for permission to take notes or tape the interview. Explain that the purpose of the tape is to help you remember what was said.
6. Be sure you have a written list of questions.
   a. Cluster your questions. All questions related to one topic should be asked together.
   b. Make sure you haven't asked too many yes/no questions.
   c. Ask some open-ended questions. "What do you think about . . .?"
   d. Phrase questions one or two ways in case the person does not understand the question.

134

e. You can ask for repeats. "Would you please repeat . . .?"

f. Ask follow-up questions. "Can you give me more details about . . .?" "Do you have anything else to add about . . .?"

g. If the person answers another question, steer the questions back to the topic. "That's interesting, but could you tell me more about . . .?"

h. If the interviewee asks you personal questions which you do not wish to answer, you can decline. "I would really rather not answer that question."

i. If the interviewee seems uncomfortable, ask him about it. "Are my questions too personal?" "Is this hard for you to talk about?" If the answer is yes, ask less personal questions.

7. When you are done with the interview, thank the interviewee for the time he/she spent with you.

After the Interview

Follow up the interview by sending the person a thank-you note.

Example:

Date

Dear _____:

Thank you for meeting with me on _____. The information you gave me was very helpful. I have enclosed a copy of my paper.

Sincerely,

Name

REFERENCE SECTION

Selected Annotated Bibliography and References

JANET C. CONSTANTINIDES
University of Wyoming

The works listed below were chosen because they have been used successfully by me and others in setting up cross-cultural awareness workshops or in adding a significant cross-cultural component to an ESL program or class. Most of them are readily accessible to the relative beginner. Those which are appropriate only for someone who has had significant experience in this area are so noted.

I feel compelled to add a strong word of caution: Many exercises or activities which are suggested for cross-cultural awareness training involve the participants in activities which focus on differences in values, beliefs, attitudes, and world views. The communication of these differences often results in threatening and defensive behavior. If the activity or exercise is not handled carefully, it may have an importantly negative effect. Consequently, I submit that those who wish to include a cross-cultural component in an ESL program or class must have first carefully planned that component, taking into account not only the intended outcomes but also the possibilities for the component to produce negative reactions and results. Cross-cultural experiences are potentially very powerful. To approach them in any but the most serious manner is, in my opinion, extremely dangerous. Any person who wishes to act as a cross-cultural trainer must first of all have realized what it is be intercultural personally. Thus I have included some works here on the definition and meaning of "cross-cultural."

The following list is by no means complete. It contains only materials which I know have been used with success.

Theory and Background

The following two books are the ones that I consider to be most useful, especially for the person new or relatively new to the area. Both provide an

137

excellent introduction to the field of cross-cultural communication, especially as it impacts on the educational process.

Althen, Gary, ed. 1981. *Learning across cultures: Intercultural communication and international educational exchange*, Washington, D.C.: National Association for Foreign Student Affairs. ERIC Document Reproduction Service No. 208 790.

This material is a must for anyone new to the field. It contains chapters on the dynamics of cross-cultural adjustment, cross-cultural counseling, English language teaching, communication and problem-solving across cultures, learning concepts and theories, and learning styles, as well as examples of how to involve foreign students in providing cross-cultural learning for Americans. There are excellent bibliographies at the ends of the chapters.

Pusch, Margaret D., ed. 1979. *Multicultural education: A cross cultural training approach*. La Grange Park, Ill: Intercultural Network.

Originally designed for faculty in teacher education programs, this is another invaluable resource for ESL teachers and administrators. The discussions of the theory of intercultural communication and the definitions of culture and class are among the most readable available. The section on teacher training provides suggestions which can be adapted to in-service training for ESL faculty. There are also some teaching strategies and evaluation procedures. Most valuable of all is the excellent annotated bibliography.

Another work which many people have found useful, especially as a good introduction to the area of cross-cultural learning, is the following one. Several articles from this work are cited in the foregoing chapters, attesting to both its worth and its readability.

Brislin, R.W., ed. 1977. *Culture learning: Concepts, applications and research*. Hawaii: East-West Center.

As the title indicates, this collection of articles originally published in *Topics in Culture Learning* plus three others is divided into three sections: (1) "Conceptualization of issues in culture learning"; (2) "Formal educational programs"; and (3) "Empirical research."

Training

Most ESL programs need to provide some cross-cultural training for the faculty and staff. If you are considering designing and carrying out your own training program, the following books are a good place to begin. Again, I want to issue a warning: Exercises and experiences used in cross-cultural training can be very disturbing, even threatening, for some people. They should be used only by people who are cognizant of the dangers and prepared to deal with them. Anyone particularly interested in cross-cultural training should be aware of the Society for Intercultural Education, Training, and Research (SIETAR, c/o Diane L. Zeller, Ph.D., 1414 22nd St. N.W., Washington, D.C. 20037).

Casse, Pierre. 1981. *Training for the cross-cultural mind.* Washington, D.C.: The Society for Intercultural Education, Training, and Research (SIETAR).

This work contains numerous exercises which can be used in cross-cultural training. Some are aimed at those new to the idea of cultural differences; others are meant for the cross-culturally sophisticated and should be used with care. A model training program is outlined.

Weeks, William H., et al. 1977. *Manual of structured experiences for cross-cultural learning.* Washington, D.C.: SIETAR.

This manual contains 59 structured exercises which pertain to initial group experiences, dynamics of communication, clarification of values, identification of roles, group process, recognition of feelings and attitudes, community interaction, brainstorming tasks and problems, and multiple objectives. Many will be useful in providing in-service training for ESL faculty; others may be adapted to use in the ESL program or class.

Classroom Activities

In addition to the those activities given in Section III of this volume, two more sources follow for activities which can be used or easily adapted to most any ESL classroom.

Donahue, Meghan and Adelaide H. Parsons. 1982. The use of roleplay to overcome cultural fatigue. *TESOL Quarterly*, Vol. 16, No. 3 (September), 359–365.

Roleplay develops an empathetic atmosphere and teaches conversation rules; it also permits members of a group to work together, make objective observations, recognize and accept differences in cultures, adapt to a new culture without losing identity, and articulate appropriate questions and statements in a given situation. This article defines cultural fatigue and discusses eight steps of roleplay (warm-up through summary) with purposes and procedures for each step.

Gaston, Jan. 1984. *Cultural awareness teaching techniques.* Brattleboro, Vt.: Pro Lingua Associates.

This "text" contains 20 "techniques," arranged according to states in intercultural adjustment, which the author developed for use in an intensive English program. There is a good introduction, setting the context for the use of the techniques. Many contain suggestions for follow-up activities using discussion, role plays, skits, or writing assignments. They need a culturally sensitive and aware teacher for successful use.

Materials on Specific Cultures

One area of great concern in providing cross-cultural information in an ESL classroom is knowing something about the cultures from which our students come. The references below, though by no means complete, provide some beginning points for gathering information about various cultures.

Donovan, Katherine C. 1981. *Assisting students and scholars from the People's Republic of China: A handbook for community groups.* Washington, D.C.: National Association for Foreign Student Affairs. ERIC Document Reproduction Service No. ED 213 616.

This monograph gives the background of attitudes, expectations, and profiles of students. It describes how to organize a community program and gives examples of specific programs: greeting, housing, food shopping, banking, etc. There is a guide to the pronunciation of Chinese names, a brief history, and a list of international student services and organizations working in specific areas for U.S.-Chinese relations. It also includes a reading list. Much of this information is adaptable to the ESL program or course.

Fieg, J. and J. Blair. 1975. *There is a difference: 12 intercultural perspectives.* Washington, D.C.: Meridian House International.

Included are capsulized discussions of the points of cultural differences between Americans and persons from Brazil, India, Japan, Kenya, Turkey, Colombia, Indonesia, Ethiopia, Jamaica, Iran, Egypt, and Nigeria. In addition to being a good source for specific information which might be used in cross-cultural awareness workshops or activities, it also contains very perceptive analyses of American culture as well.

Kitao, Kenji. 1979. *Difficulty of intercultural communication between Americans and Japanese.* Doshiva University, Kyoto: Doshiva Literature No. 29. ERIC Document Reproduction Service No. ED 191 328.

This work discusses specific cultural differences which inhibit understanding between the two cultures in terms of signs and associations with them. It provides examples of activities (i.e., breakfast), idioms, and communication patterns as well as value systems which are culturally related. Culture determines how much speakers reveal of themselves in topics of conversation and ways of self-expression. Japanese sometimes feel communicatively invaded while Americans are annoyed at the prospect of never getting past the formalities. Included are examples of differences in the ideas of physical contact, time, place, human relations, tone of voice, and sex.

Parker, O. 1976. *Cultural clues to the Middle Eastern student.* Washington, D.C.: AMIDEAST.

This work does exactly what the title promises it will: it provides social and cultural background and characteristics of students from the Middle East. AMIDEAST publishes a number of very good materials about the Middle East, including a book on the educational systems of 18 Middle Eastern countries. For information, write AMIDEAST, Information Services, Box 3, 1100 17th Street, N.W., Washington, D.C. 20036.

Stewart. E.C. 1972. *American cultural patterns: A cross-cultural perspective.* Washington, D.C.: Society for Intercultural Education, Training, and Research.

One problem many of us have in working in cross-cultural situations is being aware of and understanding our own culture. This book gives a good foundation in that area.

Other Sources of Interest

DeArmond, Murray M., M.D. 1983. Mental health and international students. *NAFSA Newsletter*, Vol. 34, No. 6 (April/May, 1983), 137ff.

Because ESL teachers deal most directly with international students, it is important to be able to serve as an "early warning system" for potential problems. This article uses three case studies to illustrate how personal problems and cultural disorientation can lead to physical problems, the causes of which may be particular to foreign students. Ability to recognize these problems can be very useful to the ESL teacher. Suggestions are made for dealing with such cases, including how the ESL teacher can help.

Heaton, James. 1978. Teaching culture as a second language: Private culture and kinesics. English Department (ESL), University of California, Los Angeles, Calif.

This paper describes video documentary techniques developed to help foreign students be aware of culture-specific nonverbal communication or body motion (kinesics) and social and personal space (proxemics). It describes an American repertoire of eyebrow positions, mouth positions, types of nods, hand motions, etc. which occur with speech. It also references video lessons various people have put together to illustrate cross-cultural nonverbal communication.

References

Adelman, M.B. and D.R. Levine. 1980. *Beyond language*. Englewood Cliffs, N.J.: Prentice-Hall.

Adler, R.B. and G. Rodman. 1985. *Understanding human communication*, 2nd ed. New York: Holt, Rinehart and Winston.

Akiyama, C. 1981. *Acceptance to zeal: Functional dialogues for students of English*. New York: Minerva Books, Ltd.

Althen, G. 1970. *Human relations training and foreign students*. Washington, D.C.: National Association for Foreign Student Affairs. ERIC Document Reproduction Service No. 048 084.

————, ed. 1978 *Students from the Arab world and Iran*. Washington, D.C.: National Association for Foreign Student Affairs.

————, ed. 1981. *Learning across cultures: Intercultural communication and international educational exchange*. Washington, D.C.: National Association for Foreign Student Affairs. ERIC Document Reproduction Service No. ED 208 790.

Bagnole, J.W. 1976. *TEFL, perceptions and the Arab world*. Washington, D.C.: American Friends of the Middle East.

Bailey, K., F. Pialorsi, and J. Zukowski/Faust, eds. 1984. *Foreign teaching assistants in U.S. universities*. Washington, D.C.: National Association for Foreign Student Affairs.

Barna, L. 1982. Stumbling blocks in intercultural communication. In L.A. Samovar and R.E. Porter (eds.), *Intercultural communication: A reader*, 3rd ed. Belmont, Calif.: Wadsworth.

Barnlund, D.C. 1975. *Public and private self in Japan and the United States*. Tokyo: Simul Press.

Barzini, L. 1971. *From Caesar to the Mafia: Sketches of Italian life*. New York: The Library Press.

Beneke, J. 1981. Cultural monsters, mimicry, and English as an international language. In R. Freudenstein, J. Beneke, and H. Ponisch (eds.), *Language incorporated: Teaching foreign language in industry*. Oxford: Pergamon Press.

Bochner, S. 1977. The mediating man and cultural diversity. In R.W. Brislin (ed.), *Culture learning: Concepts, applications and research*. Hawaii: East-West Center.

Brein, M. and K.H. David. 1971. Intercultural communication and adjustment of the sojourner. *Psychological Bulletin* 76:215–230.

Brislin, R.W., ed. 1977. *Culture learning: Concepts, applications and research*. Hawaii: East-West Center.

_____1981. *Cross-cultural encounters*. New York: Pergamon Press.

Brislin, R.W. and P. Pedersen. 1976. *Cross-cultural orientation programs*. New York: Gardner Press.

Brophy, J. and T.L. Good. 1974. *Teacher-student relationships: Causes and consequences*. New York: Holt, Rinehart and Winston.

Brooks, N.D. 1968. Teaching culture in the foreign language classroom. *Foreign Language Annals* 1:204–217.

Brown, H.D. 1977. Some limitations of C-L/CLL models of second language teaching. *TESOL Quarterly* ll:365–372.

Carley, D. 1982. *Dynamics of intercultural communication*. Dubuque, Iowa: William C. Brown.

Casse, P. 1979. *Training for the cross-cultural mind*. Washington, D.C.: Society for Intercultural Education, Training, and Research.

Cazden, C.B. and V.P. John. 1971. Learning in American Indian children. In M.L. Wax, S. Diamond, and F.O. Gearing (eds.), *Anthropological perspectives on education*. New York: Basic Books, Inc.

Chastain, K. 1976. *Developing second-language skills: Theory to practice*, 2nd ed. Chicago: Rand-McNally.

Clark, H. 1975. Bridging. In R.C. Schank and B.L. Nash-Webber (eds.), *Theoretical issues in natural language processing*. Proceedings of an interdisciplinary workshop, Cambridge, Mass., June 10–13.

Condon, J. and M. Saito. 1974. *Intercultural encounters with Japan: Communication, contact and conflict*. Tokyo: Simul Press.

Condon, J. and F. Yousef. 1975. *An introduction to intercultural communication*. Indianapolis: Bobbs-Merrill.

142

Conrad, A.W. and J.A. Fishman. 1977. English as a world language: the evidence. In J.A. Fishman, R. Cooper, and A. Conrad (eds.), *The Spread of English*. Rowley, Mass.: Newbury House.

Corbett, E.P.J. 1971. *Classical rhetoric for the modern student*, 2nd ed. New York: Oxford University Press.

Coulmas, F., ed. 1981. *Conversational routine: Explorations in standardized communication situations and prepared speech*. The Hague: Mouton.

Curwin, R. and B.S. Fuhrman. 1975. *Discovering your teaching self: Humanistic approaches to effective speaking*. Englewood Cliffs, N.J.: Prentice-Hall.

Das, M.S. and P.D. Bardis, eds. 1978. *The family in Asia*. New Delhi: Vikas Publishing House Pvt. Ltd.

Dodd, C. 1982. *Dynamics of intercultural communication*. Dubuque, Iowa: William C. Brown.

Donahue, M. and A. H. Parsons. 1982. The use of roleplay to overcome cultural fatigue. *TESOL Quarterly* 16:359–365.

Drazdauskiene, M. 1981. On stereotypes in conversation. In F. Coulmas (ed.), *Conversational routine*. The Hague: Mouton.

Dunnett, S. 1981. English language teaching from an intercultural perspective. In G. Althen (ed.), *Learning across cultures: Intercultural communication and international educational exchange*. Washington, D.C.: National Association for Foreign Student Affairs. ERIC Document Reproduction Service No. 208 790.

Education Testing Service. 1984. *Listening to TOEFL: Test Kit 2*. Princeton, N.J..

Eiseley, L. 1971. The brown wasps. In L. Eiseley, *The night country*. New York: Charles Scribner's Sons.

Elbow, P. 1973. *Writing without teachers*. New York: Oxford University Press.

Fisher, G. 1979. *American communication in a global society*. Norwood, N.J.: Ablex Publishing Corporation.

Foust, S., ed. 1981. Dynamics of cross-cultural adjustment: From pre-arrival to re-entry. In G. Althen (ed.), *Learning across cultures: Intercultural communication and international educational exchange*. Washington, D.C.: National Association for Foreign Student Affairs. ERIC Document Reproduction Service No. ED 208 790.

Freeman, H. and N.R. Kurtz, eds. 1969. *America's trouble*. Englewood Cliffs, N.J.: Prentice-Hall.

Garcia, R. 1984. Countering classroom discrimination. *Theory into Practice* 23:104–109.

Garreau, J. 1982. *Nine nations of North America*. New York: Avon Books.

Glenn, E.S., D. Witmeyer, and K.A. Stevenson. 1977. Cultural styles of persuasion. *International Journal of Intercultural Relations* 3:132–148.

Glenn, E.S. with C.G. Glenn. 1981. *Man and mankind: Conflict and communication between cultures*. Norwood, N.J.: Ablex Publishing Corp.

Gochenour, T. 1977. Is experiential learning something fundamentally different? In D. Batchelder and E.G. Warner (eds.), *Beyond experience: The experiential approach to cross-cultural education.* Brattleboro, Vt.: The Experiment Press.

Gochenour, T. and A. Janeway. 1977. Seven concepts in cross-cultural interaction. In D. Batchelder and E.G. Warner (eds.), *Beyond experience: The experiential approach to cross-cultural education.* Brattleboro, Vt.: The Experiment Press.

Gregg, J.Y. 1981. *Communication and culture.* Belmont, Calif.: Wadsworth Publishing Co.

Grice, H. 1975. Logic and conversation. In P. Cole and J. Morgan (eds.), *Syntax and semantics,* Vol. 3. New York: Academic Press.

Grimshaw, A.D. 1981. *Language as a social resource.* Stanford: Stanford University Press.

Grove, C.L. 1977. The cross-cultural problems of immigrant Portuguese students in American schools. ERIC Document No. ED 151 472.

Gudykunst, W. and Y. Kim, eds. 1984. *Methods for intercultural communication.* Beverly Hills, Calif.: Sage Publications.

Gumperz, J. 1978. The conversational analysis of inter-ethnic communication. In E. Ross (ed.), *Inter-ethnic communication.* Athens, Ga.: University of Georgia Press.

———1982. *Discourse strategies.* Cambridge: Cambridge University Press.

Guthrie, G.M. 1975. A behavioral analysis of culture learning. In R.W. Brislin, S. Bochner, and W.J. Lonner (eds.), *Cross-cultural perspectives on learning.* New York: John Wiley and Sons.

Hakuta, K. 1976. A case study of a Japanese child learning English as a second language. *Language Learning* 26:321–352.

Hall, E.T. 1966. *The silent language.* Garden City, N.Y.: Anchor Press, Doubleday.

———1976. *Beyond culture.* Garden City, N.Y.: Anchor Books.

Halliday, M.A.K. 1978. *Language as a social semiotic.* Baltimore: University Park Press.

Harris, L. and Associates, Inc. 1975. *The myth and reality of aging in America.* Washington, D.C.: The National Council on Aging, Inc.

Harris, P.R. and R.T. Moran. 1979. *Managing cultural differences* (The International Management Productivity Series, Vol. 1). Houston, Texas: Gulf Publishing Company.

Harrison, L. 1984. A project evaluation. Student term paper, Guilford College, Greensboro, N.C.

Hatch, E. 1978. *Second language acquisition.* Rowley, Mass.: Newbury House.

Henry, J. 1976. A cross-cultural outline of education. In J.I. Roberts and S.K. Akinsanya (eds.), *Educational patterns and cultural configurations: The anthropology of education.* New York: David McKay Company, Inc.

Hoopes, D.S. 1979. Introduction: Notes on the evolution of cross-cultural training. In D.S. Hoopes and P. Ventura (eds.), *Intercultural sourcebook: Cross-cultural training methodologies.* Chicago: Intercultural Press.

144

Hoopes, D.S. and P. Ventura, eds. 1979. *Intercultural sourcebook: Cross-cultural training methodologies*. Chicago: Intercultural Press.

Hsu, F.C.K. 1969. *The study of literate civilizations* (Studies in Anthropological Methods Series). New York: Holt, Rinehart and Winston.

Hughes, G.H. 1984. An argument for culture analysis in the second language classroom. *The American Language Journal II* 1:31–51.

Hymes, D. 1972. Models of the interaction of language and social life. In J. Gumperz and D. Hymes (eds.), *Directions in sociolinguistics*. New York: Holt, Rinehart and Winston.

Irving, K.J. 1984. Cross-cultural awareness and the ESL classroom. *Theory into Practice* 23:138–143.

Jackson, P.W. 1968. *Life in classrooms*. New York: Holt, Rinehart and Winston.

Jaramillo, M. 1973. Cultural differences in ESOL classrooms. *TESOL Quarterly* 7:51–60.

Jenkins, H.M., ed. 1983. *Educating students from other nations*. San Francisco: Jossey-Bass.

Johnson, J. 1979. *Living language*. Rowley, Mass.: Newbury House.

Johnson, J.A. 1983. *Writing strategies for ESL students*. New York: MacMillan.

Jones, L. and C. von Baeyer. 1984. *Functions of American English: Communicative activities for the classroom*. Cambridge: Cambridge University Press.

Kaplan, A. 1970. *Individuality and the new society*. Seattle: University of Washington Press.

Kearny, E.N., M.A. Kearny, and J. Crandall. 1984. *The American way*. Englewood Cliffs, N.J.: Prentice-Hall.

Keller, E. and S.T. Warner. 1976–79. *Gambits: Conversation tools*. Ottawa: The Ministry of Supply and Services, Canada.

————1980a. *Gambits: Links*. Quebec: Canadian Government Publishing Centre.

————1980b. *Gambits: Openings*. Quebec: Canadian Government Publishing Centre.

Kramsch, C.J. 1981a. *Discourse analysis and second language teaching*. Washington, D.C.: Center for Applied Linguistics.

————1981b. Teaching discussion skills: A pragmatic approach. *Foreign Language Annals* 14:93–104.

Krashen, S. 1981. *Second language acquisition and second language learning*. Oxford: Pergamon Press.

Kroeber, A.L. and C. Kluckhohn. 1963. *Culture: A critical review of concepts and definitions*. New York: Vintage Books.

Lafayette, R.C. 1979. *Teaching culture: Strategies and techniques* (Language in Education Series, No. 11). Arlington, Va.: Center for Applied Linguistics.

Laver, J. 1981. Linguistic routines and politeness in greeting and parting. In F. Coulmas (ed.), *Conversational routine*. The Hague: Mouton.

Lawrence, M. 1972. *Writing as a thinking process*. Ann Arbor, Mich.: University of Michigan Press.

145

Lee, H. 1960. *To kill a mockingbird*. Philadelphia: J.B. Lippincott.

Lee, M.Y., M. Abd-Ella, and L.A. Burks. 1981. *Needs of foreign students from developing nations at U.S. colleges and universities*. Washington, D.C.: National Association for Foreign Student Affairs.

Lee, W.R. 1983. *A dictionary of social English*. Oxford: Pergamon Press.

Levine, D.R. and M.B. Adelman. 1982. *Beyond language*. Englewood Cliffs, N.J.: Prentice-Hall.

Lewis, B. 1982. *The Muslim discovery of Europe*. New York: W.W. Norton and Company.

Louv, R. *America II*. 1983. Los Angeles: Jeremy P. Tarcher, Inc.

Loveday, L. 1982. *The sociolinguistics of learning and using a non-native language*. Oxford: Pergamon Press.

Macrorie, K. 1970. *Telling writing*. Rochelle Park, N.J.: Hayden Publishers.

Maslow, A.H. 1954. *Motivation and personality*. New York: Harper and Row.

McLeod, B. 1980. The relevance of anthropology to language teaching. In K. Croft (ed.), *Readings on English as a second language*. Boston: Little, Brown and Company.

Michener, J. 1975. *Reader's Digest*. August. Page 99.

Minsky, M. 1975. A framework for representing knowledge. In P.H. Winston (ed.), *The psychology of computer vision*. New York: McGraw-Hill.

Oberg, K. 1979. Culture shock and the problem of adjustment in new cultural environments. In E.C. Smith and L.F. Luce (eds.), *Toward internationalism*. Rowley, Mass.: Newbury House.

Ouchi, W. G. 1981. *Theory Z: How American business can meet the challenge*. Reading, Mass.: Addison-Wesley.

Parker, O.D. 1976. *Cultural clues to the Middle Eastern student*. Washington, D.C.: American Friends of the Middle East.

Parlett, M. and D. Hamilton. 1972. Evaluation as illumination: A new approach to the study of innovatory processes. Occasional paper. Centre for Research in the Educational Sciences, University of Edinburgh.

Patai, R. 1983. *The Arab mind*. New York: Charles Scribner's Sons.

Paulston, C.B. 1975. Linguistic and communicative competence. *TESOL Quarterly* 8:347–362.

————1978. Biculturalism: some reflections and speculations. *TESOL Quarterly* 12:369–380.

Pfeiffer, J. W. and J.E. Jones, ed. 1970–85. *A handbook of structured experiences for human relations training*, Vols. I-X. La Jolla, Calif.: University Associates.

Philips, S. 1972. Participant structures and communicative competence: Warm Springs children in community and classroom. In C.B. Cazden, V.P. John, and D. Hymes (eds.), *Functions of language in the classroom*. New York: Teachers College Press.

Pusch, M.C., ed. 1979. *Multicultural education: A cross cultural training approach*. Chicago: Intercultural Press.

Redden, W. 1975. *Culture shock inventory—manual*. Fredericton, N.B., Canada: Organizational Tests Ltd.

146

Richards, J. 1980. Conversation. *TESOL Quarterly* 14:413–432.

Robinett, B.W. 1978. *Teaching English to speakers of other languages: Substance and technique.* New York: McGraw-Hill.

Rogers, C. 1951. *Client-centered therapy.* Boston: Houghton Mifflin.

————1961. *On becoming a person.* Boston: Houghton Mifflin.

Ruhly, S. 1976. *Orientations to intercultural communication.* Chicago: Science Research Associates, Inc.

Russo, G.M. 1983. *Expanding communication: Teaching modern languages at the college level.* New York: Harcourt, Brace, Jovanovich.

Sajavaara, K. and J. Lehtonen. 1978. *Spoken language and the concept of fluency.* ERIC Document Reproduction Service No. ED 158 600.

Samovar, L.A. and R.E. Porter. 1976. *Intercultural communication: A reader.* Belmont, Calif.: Wadsworth Publishing.

Sapir, E. 1949. *Selected writings in language, culture and personality.* Ed. by D.C. Mandelbaum. Berkeley and Los Angeles: University of California Press.

Saville-Troike, M. 1976. *Foundations for teaching English as a second langauge: Theory and method for multicultural education.* Englewood Cliffs, N.J.: Prentice-Hall.

Schumann, J.H. 1978. The acculturation model for second-language acquisition. In R. Gingras (ed.), *Second-language acquisition and foreign language teaching.* Washington, D.C.: Center for Applied Linguistics.

Seelye, H.N. 1968. *Analysis and teaching of cross-cultural context* (Britannica Review of Foreign Language Education, Vol. 1). Chicago: Encyclopaedia Britannica.

————1974. *Teaching culture: Strategies for foreign language educators.* Skokie, Ill.: National Textbook Company.

Sevareid, E. 1964. *This is Eric Sevareid.* New York: McGraw-Hill.

Shimahara, N. 1978. Socialization for college entrance examinations in Japan. *Comparative Education* 14:253–266.

Smith, E.C. and L.F. Luce. 1979. *Toward internationalism: Readings in cross-cultural communication.* Rowley, Mass.: Newbury House.

Smith, L.E. 1977. Teaching English in Asia—an overview. In R.W. Brislin (ed.), *Culture learning concepts, applications and research.* Hawaii: East-West Center.

Smith, N. and D. Wilson. 1979. *Modern linguistics: The results of Chomsky's revolution.* Harmondsworth: Penguin.

Srinivasan, L. 1977. *Perspectives on nonformal adult learning.* New York: World Education.

Spradley, J. 1979. *The ethnographic interview.* New York: Holt, Rinehart and Winston.

Springer, U. 1977. Education, curriculum and pedagogy. *Comparative Education Review* 12:358–369.

Stevick, E.W. 1976. *Memory, meaning and method.* Rowley, Mass.: Newbury House.

_____1980. A *way and ways*. Rowley, Mass.: Newbury House.

Stewart, E.C. 1972. *American cultural patterns: A cross-cultural perspective*. Chicago: Intercultural Press.

Stoddard, S. 1983. A case of collusion: Cultural redundancy and the allowable economies of grammar. Paper presented to the Minnesota Regional Conference on Language and Literature, Minneapolis, May 13–14.

_____1984. Domains of reference and the definite article: Implications for teaching ESL. Paper presented to International TESOL Conference, Houston, March 6–11.

Szanston, D. 1966. Cultural confrontation in the Philippines. In R. Textor (ed.), *Cultural frontiers of the Peace Corps*. Boston: MIT Press.

TESOL Newsletter. 1984. Regents survey finds most ESL teachers well experienced. 18:11

Trifonovitch, G.J. 1977. On cross-cultural orientation techniques. In R.W. Brislin (ed.), *Culture learning: Concepts, applications and research*. Hawaii: East-West Center.

Watanabe, T. 1984. Teaching Engish to Japanese students: An examination of cross-cultural differences. Unpublished manuscript. Department of General Linguistics, University of Pittsburgh.

Watson, K.A. 1977. Understanding human interaction: The study of everyday life and ordinary talk. In R.W. Brislin (ed.), *Culture learning: Concepts, applications and research*. Hawaii: East-West Center.

Wedge, B. 1968. Communication analysis and comprehensive diplomacy. In A.S. Hoffman (ed.), *International communication and the new diplomacy*. Bloomington, Ind.: Indiana University Press.

Wedge, B. and C. Muromcew. 1965. Psychological factors in Soviet disarmament negotiations. *Journal of Conflict Resolution* 9:18–36.

Weeks, W., P. Pederson, R.W. Brislin, eds. 1977. *A manual of structured experiences for cross-cultural learning*. Chicago: Intercultural Press.

Widdowson, H.G. 1979. *Explorations in applied linguistics*. New York: Oxford University Press.

Whorf, B.L. 1956. *Language, thought and reality: Selected writings*. Ed. by J.B. Carrol. Cambridge, Mass.: MIT Press, and New York: Wiley.

Wolff, M. 1968. *The house of Lim*. New York: Appleton-Century-Crofts.

Yorio, C.A. 1980. Conventional language forms and the development of communicative competence. *TESOL Quarterly* 14:433–442.

NOTES

About the Editors

Patricia Byrd has been chair of the Department of English as a Second Language at Georgia State University since 1985. Previously, she was assistant director of the Intensive English Program at the University of Florida for ten years. In both positions, one of her goals has been to incorporate cross-cultural orientation and training into ESL programs and into programs that train ESL teachers.

Janet C. Constantinides is assistant chair of the Department of English at the University of Wyoming. She has been a cross-cultural trainer for eight years and has designed and presented workshops in cross-cultural communication for faculty and staff, and for ESL students, including foreign teaching assistants. She has developed a series of videotapes for use in cross-cultural awareness workshops.